THE HEART OF
FRANCE

A JOURNEY OF DISCOVERY

TEXT BY

CATHERINE CALVERT

FOREWORD BY

NANCY LINDEMEYER

HEARST BOOKS
NEW YORK

AUTHOR'S ACKNOWLEDGMENTS:

With gratitude to Nancy Lindemeyer for
her vision of the world, and to my family,
my patient traveling companions.

Library of Congress Cataloging-in-Publication Data

The heart of France.
              p.   cm.
        Includes index.
        ISBN 0-688-17438-8
        1. France Guidebooks.   I. Hearst
Books (Firm)
    DC16.H43   2000
    914.404'84--dc21   99-36640
                                         CIP

Printed in Hong Kong
This book is set in Janson

FIRST EDITION

10   9   8   7   6   5   4   3   2   1

For *Victoria* magazine:
Nancy Lindemeyer, Editor in Chief
Eliette Markhbein, European Editor
Susan Maher, Art Director

www.williammorrow.com • www.victoriamag.com

Editor: Jodi Brandon
Designer: Susi Oberhelman
Produced by Smallwood & Stewart, Inc.,
New York City

CONTENTS

FOREWORD

What a privilege it is to be in France. How carefully its people have guarded their homes, their gardens, their cuisine. It is all there to rediscover endlessly. When I think of France, I think not only of the parks of Paris and the gracious country châteaux. I think of the First of May and the little bouquet of lily of the valley in every child's hand; I recall the wonderful home cooking with vegetables and herbs fresh from the garden; I relish the pair of red satin shoes I bought in a pretty shop. The French have a way of doing things that is just about perfect. It is seldom pretentious; it is always about elegance, artistry, and simplicity. I wonder why we all can't have this élan, but it seems to be their special gift.

It is a gift that resides at the heart of France, as we discover in this book. It is what allows the French to tarry in a café or stroll through the wisteria without destination; to infuse their lives with the nectar of roses, whether by the gardenful or by a drop of perfume; to be chic without ever trying. Throughout the country we find much that is momentous, much that is discreet, and much that is still a mystery. I hope that you will join us on these beautiful pages and be guided by their spirit as you take this land to your heart.

Nancy Lindemeyer
Editor in Chief

INTRODUCTION

hink of France, and the images rush in, each as evocative as a fine perfume: An evening in Brittany, with a table of shellfish, a dish of melted butter, and a bottle of crisp wine, appetites heightened after a day walking long empty beaches. An afternoon in a market in the south of France, your basket filled with a pair of newly bought espadrilles, some cheese wrapped in green leaves, and a few bars of lavender soap. Late night in a Paris restaurant, ribbons of light illuminating the streets. At dusk, an amble down a country lane lined with larches, where every bend in the road reveals another small gray stone house, bright with window boxes

At Château de Vault-de-Lugny, time has lent a lovely patina to the old masonry.

A TOWN HALL COURTYARD IN ALSACE

cling along, carrying baguettes under their arms, and women who are so simply dressed yet so chic that the onlooker immediately feels dowdy. Beyond the obvious icons, though, the search for France takes subtler turns. North to south, east to west, in vibrant cities and in country villages, the exploration offers access to a world that has attracted and charmed visitors for hundreds of years with its style and substance. The art of living is practiced here as nowhere else—a finely polished art that demands much attention and is of prime importance in the French view of life. The curious visitor becomes the beneficiary of the fine food, elegant

spilling geraniums. A morning in a cathedral, the windows casting lacy shadows on the old tombs, the sound of the choir practicing and the mumble of prayers providing a backdrop.

France is a conundrum, a country of paradoxes, of contrasting scenes and sensibilities; discovering all her many faces can be a life's work, full of delicious expeditions from one end of this sizable country to the other. Of course, there are prototypical Frenchmen sporting berets and bicy-

A STATUARY IN PARIS'S BAGATELLE

ers in the Dordogne? For hundreds of years, virtually nothing, which meant that each region found its own ways. Today we savor the differences, whether it's a wine grown only in Burgundy, a fabric bright with sunny prints that reflects Provence, a cake that requires Norman apples, or a wallpaper that's still made as it was two centuries ago in Alsace. Each province, each *département*, can seem fiercely independent, proud of its traditions and customs, and unique down to the shape of the local bread.

At the heart of it all—geographically and figuratively—lies Paris. (Distances throughout the

shop windows, picturesque streets lined with glorious architecture—all a reminder of what hundreds of years of concern with detail can do to further the cause of civilization.

In the broad expanses that are France, where traces of historic divisions, both political and military, still shadow the landscape, regionalism lives. As with the rest of the world, isolation once meant separate languages and customs from one end of the country to the other. After all, what did the Breton-speaking, fish-eating Celts of Brittany have to do with the Champagne makers in Reims or the farm-

IN THE CHAMPAGNE CELLARS NEAR REIMS

country are measured from the square in front of the Cathedral of Notre-Dame, so the city is literally the center.) Paris can be disparaged for its big-city ways—the hustle and bustle, the crisp manners, the anonymity—but it is truly the source of everything new, the place where creative sparks fly and where innovators settle and work together. Still, this is a city of small neighborhoods, where simply crossing the river or walking ten minutes can take you from the immaculately turned-out children and trim young mothers of the 8th arrondissement to the university students deep in conversation in the Latin Quarter. Such disparities

PARIS FLOWER SHOP CARREFOUR DE L'ODÉON

FANCIFUL ANTIQUE PERFUME BOTTLES

make wandering in Paris a constant joy, with each corner framing a vista that beckons the walker on, whether it's the crooked cobblestone streets or the riverbanks where lovers embrace and the bateaux-mouches take the long slow curve around Notre-Dame. Paris is about discovery, from a painting seen in a new light to a boutique that sells lemon- and lavender-scented linens.

It has been said that France is everyone's second country, and perhaps it is the country that we would create if we had time and energy enough. That sublime French style, which seems to beckon to each of us, is all about choosing a little of what is absolutely excellent rather than a lot of what's nearly right. It is something instilled in French children practically from birth, when they are dressed in clothing that is as practical as anywhere on earth but somehow infinitely more tasteful. The

A MANUSCRIPT AT THE MUSÉE COLETTE

FIELD FLOWERS FROM THE SOUTH OF FRANCE

cut of a collar or the drape of a dress is a matter of serious consideration; a little girl goes off to school with an enveloping coverall so that her perfect little dress is unmarred. Since children are part of the adults' world from the first, manners are an important issue from the earliest years—manners in the grand old style, with handshakes for elders and lots of cutlery to be maneuvered at dinner.

The search for perfection extends to all aspects of life. Food must be fresh—and if that requires a daily trip to the market to purchase the

enough to convince many that the French flair for design might have started before there was paper!) At the other end of the scale, a Frenchwoman is willing to visit a dozen shops to find the perfect blue blazer, for instance, and invest substantial money in it, knowing that this classic will serve her well for years. Shops are dazzling in their temptations, with the simplest item—soap perhaps, or writing paper—displayed in such a way that it looks completely new to us. Such a passion for all that makes up the visible glories of life comes to the dinner table each night, and that love of well-

tomatoes and discuss the lamb, then so be it. Furnishing a house until it's just full enough of an artful assemblage of fine antiques and proper lengths of fabric is a skill that results in harmony at home. And fashion is never far away, even at the cheapest levels: Visit a store like Monoprix, a chain of inexpensive shops, and marvel at how well designed the dinnerware is, how stylish the clothing. (A look at the cave paintings of Lascaux is

A PARISIAN QUILT SHOP

of the language—French properly spoken with all its nuances, though struggling at times against the pop-speak of English—remain important aspects of every French child's heritage. Novelists and poets are respected members of society, and television is filled daily with serious discussions that command large audiences. Certainly there's small talk, but there's a preponderance of great talk, too, at the dinner table and in the press.

A PRECIOUS EXAMPLE OF FINE FRENCH HANDWORK

prepared food is where many of us have experienced the French appetite for perfection—quite literally. Though there are those who experiment with technique and others who might go out for Chinese food or try a Moroccan restaurant, for the rest of us it's dining in the classic French way, whether at a cozy bistro where we tuck into perfect frites and a fruit tart, or at a Michelin-star-studded restaurant, where the proprietor seems to share our delight in a meal cooked with great devotion and served up with a flourish.

The French desire for perfection extends to the life of the mind as well. The love of philosophy,

A fine sense of the past underlies much of what constitutes France today. Part of the glory of France resides in its political and historical heritage, with reminders of many invaders and of many lost kingdoms and tribes to be discovered. Look closely at the beauty of the old villages, where time has rubbed off the stones' rough edges and daily life has worn a path from boulangerie to café, and you will feel a sense of the eternal from this mundane brush with history. The spectacle of the past is as easy to visit as the ordinary: Go to Chartres during a mass and watch the pilgrims

A SHOP IN NORMANDY, WHERE THE APPLE IS KING

DINNER IN A PROVENÇAL GARDEN

filled with hope, the stained glass tempering the light like a dream. The respect for tradition, for things-as-they-have-been-done, is a strong undercurrent in family life as well, whether it's something as simple as a recipe or as lavish as an ancestral château passed down from generation to generation. Though it is said that the French are in search of their identity again, uncertain what to make of their place in modern Europe or of the temptations that come from abroad—fast food is a good example—they stand firm on the bedrock of a love and knowledge of the past. For those of us who turn to France for another look at what human hands and human hearts can do to bring out the best in life, time spent here is a revelation never to be forgotten. Certain memories will never fade, however small, tucked away in the back of the mind: the *clunk* of a ball as it hits another in a game

A SIMPLE BISTRO IN A SMALL VILLAGE

THE RICHNESS OF CHOICE AT A CHEESE SHOP

of pétanque under the trees of a Provençal square as a long summer's evening dwindles away; the light in the Fontainebleau forest just as the Impressionists captured it a hundred years ago; the wine and the wild strawberries with a cloud of cream sampled one May day; the dress for a little girl that made her a momentary angel. And always the hours strolling through the streets of Paris, when every turn brought revelation.

TRADITION

IKE A RICH TAPESTRY, FINELY

WOVEN, TOO PRECIOUS TO DISCARD,

THE PAST IS ALWAYS PART

OF THE PRESENT IN FRANCE, WHERE

WHAT IS MODERN LIVES PEACEFULLY

WITH THE BEST OF WHAT

HAS GONE BEFORE. AT HOME, IN CITIES,

TOWNS, AND VILLAGES, THE

TIMELESS TREASURES OF THE PAST ARE

A MATTER FOR EVERY DAY.

HOSPITALITY

hey're some of our most romantic images

of France—those turreted towers and steep pitched

roofs that crown the hilltops or sit in broad expanses of

green fields. The châteaux of France are what fantasy is

all about—the story of Cinderella is, after all, a French

fairy tale, and these castles are just the sort of place in

which she'd choose to live. Many of them have been

able to preserve a sense of intimacy and family living

Château de Louvignies in Belgium is a legacy of French design.

even in the midst of great splendor. As everywhere in Europe, the roots of these grand buildings lie far in the past, in the fortresses that were built in medieval times to defend roads, rivers, and sometimes whole domains, and many of these remain—at least judging from their outward appearance—as grim as clenched fists, with thick walls and narrow windows, shut off from the world. But a large number of the finest were built during the Renaissance, in that flowering of art and architecture that seemed to follow Marie de Médicis from Italy in the seventeenth century. There were— and are—châteaux of all descriptions: some small and simple, others enormous engines of display and magnificence, like Versailles, which was a veritable stage set for the high drama that was court life beginning in the mid-seventeenth century. The Loire valley is particularly rich in châteaux, as it was an area that was long a country retreat for royals and nobles. The fairy-tale qualities of the one at Azay-le-Rideau, for instance, have been enchanting visitors for

In Eugénie-les-Bains, opposite, spa-goers have enjoyed the restorative waters since Napoleon's time. Les Prés d'Eugénie, above and below, is an elegant retreat for those in search of peace and pampering.

BRETON WELCOME

Tradition is the watchword on the coast of Brittany, especially at the Hôtel Printania in Dinard, where staff still wear the starched caps and decorated aprons once so common in the region. The hotel shines with the attentiveness of three generations of the Ribaucourt family. The grandparents of the current owners created the hotel by joining three seaside houses and filling them with the painted furniture and upholstered chairs typical of old Brittany, then added their own warm welcome. The collection remains unique, displayed at every turn—on one cupboard nailheads spell out the date 1885, while other panels are used to decorate the lofty dining room, left, where portraits of women in their lacy Breton caps remind visitors of earlier days.

Guests have their own traditions, returning again and again, knowing that this is the place to find some of the best that the region offers: seafood cooked to perfection, then served up in the dining room; a saunter along the promenade and a concert by the village band; tea on the balcony overlooking the waves. "We're intent on keeping the old traditions alive," says Françoise de Ribaucourt. She needn't worry: That is a goal her family achieves over and over, maintaining the hotel as it always has been, full of welcome and peace.

four hundred years, and no one can resist the charms of the castle at Chenonceaux, which also dates from the Renaissance.

Many of these châteaux are still family homes, whose inhabitants have hung on through wars and revolutions, and they remain the center of family life for many. Sometimes there are enough wings and outbuildings for each generation to take a portion, and sometimes (though the process is much less extensive than in England) the doors have opened for daily visitors or paying guests. However, be assured that most things go on in the old ways, with ancient silks still covering a fine armchair and books that perhaps Voltaire read on a visit still on the shelves. Traditions are as important as the furnishings, and joys are celebrated as everywhere else on earth.

From farmhouse to villa, the rituals of daily life are valued. As in wine, food, language, and houses, regional tastes rule. Northern half-timbered houses would be out of place in the sunwashed south of France, where wide windows and

High in the French Alps, the architecture reflects the reality of nature. Pitched roofs protect from the snow, above; traditional ironwork, cow and all, decorate a window, left.

"Breton blue" decorates a thatched-roof cottage in Brittany, near where innkeeper Eric Guérin plays host to those seeking the tranquility of these little islands in the Brière. Guests enjoy the quiet of this nature preserve— and the superb cuisine in the dining room, opposite.

tiles invite the light in. High in the mountains, steep-pitched roofs provide shelter from the elements, and Belle Époque influences show up in both small towns and large cities throughout the country. The signature tall dormered mansard roof so typical of French buildings even in this century was developed by Louis XIV's architect, François Mansart, who worked on royal commissions such as Versailles.

Travelers have always sought special places to stay in France, paging through their well-worn Michelin guides or other travel books (there's even one that specializes in *relais du silence*— hotels that promise peace and quiet). Increasingly, there are choices—bed and breakfasts, guest houses, inns— that make the journey worthwhile. The search might lead to a château where an elderly countess escorts the way past ancestral portraits to a tall poster bed beneath a threadbare tapestry; or a visitor might find warmth and comfort in the mountains under a huge eiderdown, or take breakfast on a terrace surveying the lavender fields of the south. They would all be at home in France, if only for a while.

BRITTANY WEDDING

In France, celebrations about family and community are filled with traditions, rituals, and bonds that transcend the years. There is no doubt that a party for a wedding, a christening, or an anniversary will be held at home, with cousins and uncles squashed about the table or, for the more fortunate (those with more room—and blessed by good weather), a tumble of generations wandering the gardens after a luncheon or dancing under the

stars. Favorite recipes are the source for this feast; old stories told time and time again are the table talk. For the wedding in Brittany pictured here, a religious ceremony was held at the local church. Then the entire village (there were 450 guests in all) congregated at the seventeenth-century château belonging to the groom's family to witness the civil ceremony. At the wedding celebration, flowers, at their July peak, were everywhere. Guests dined on classic dishes: fish, local cheeses, foie gras, and Champagne. In step with tradition, the reception was filled with speeches—rather than shorter toasts, as in America—that might have taken days to prepare. Despite the size of the gathering, the occasion was intimate, all about family and friends: The groom's brother, a priest, performed the religious ceremony, and the attendants were all nieces and nephews of the groom. The celebration lasted well into the night, and the next day guests returned for a post-wedding feast of cider and crêpes in a ongoing tribute to the next generation joining the family line.

For years, the owners of La Maison du Bassin watched as the Atlantic Ocean wore away at the old hotel on Cap-Ferret. They dreamed of reviving it, of bringing fresh sea breezes into the old structure. Two years ago they claimed it, and now it stands shining near the shore, the eternal summer house, all polished wood and fresh white bed linens, with vases overflowing with flowers everywhere. With a nod to the past—lots of repolished antiques, the traditional rattan chairs on the ter-

BORDEAUX RETREAT

Once the province of fishermen, Cap-Ferret is now a resort for those who crave the simple life. La Maison du Bassin offers peace, quiet, fine food, and a breezy porch from which to comtemplate the sea.

race, mosquito netting in the bedrooms—this is the past recast, with nothing fusty about it. A palette of blue and white—whitewashed walls, draperies and shower curtains made of sailcloth, and snappy blue paint for details—echoes the sea. Local artists painted many of the pictures on the walls. On the terrace, guests linger over coffee served in large deep bowls with white cotton piqué napkins and homemade jams. The afternoon promises a picnic—baskets filled with delectables specially prepared by the hotel staff—or a sail, bike ride, or leisurely tour through the countryside. And dinner—who wouldn't happily settle into a twig chair in the dining room, with a plate of fresh oysters to start off a memorable meal? Life, and the sound of the sea, are always sweet here.

All roads lead to the sea in Cap-Ferret, where the Atlantic throws up restless clouds. On stormy days, thunder is best appreciated in a lace-topped bed within the cozy inn.

CRAFTSMANSHIP

t's the hand that tells the story of French luxury goods. Many talented artisans still work in the old ways, using techniques passed down from generation to generation—whether smoothing fine leather, weaving cloth, printing paper, or etching glass. The tradition of the craftsman, though perhaps diminished in modern times, is a cherished part of the French heritage, and careful shoppers are willing to spend extra

Two Hermès classics are the traveling secretary and the Kelly bag.

for goods that bear the imprint of fine work and the promise of individual attention. The hand that seeks out such things knows that just a touch will reveal their fineness. Weigh a handblown wine glass in the palm, stroke the tender leather of a handbag or suitcase, or let a silk scarf caress your skin—these are the unmistakable pleasures for those who patronize the crafts of living well.

Though their clientele and their shops are now worldwide, many French firms have long histories of catering to the wealthy who visited Paris just to furnish a wedding trousseau or fill a home with splendid objects. Open their ledgers and you'll see the names of those who traveled to France for a dose of luxury—and those who knew that the imprimatur of a French merchant like Hermès, Christofle, or Limoges would enhance the beauty of the purchase that much more. These businesses have always been mindful of their history of service to rich, royal, and discerning clientele, and have gone to great lengths to preserve—and in some cases re-create—the grand traditions of the past: great traveling

Painstaking attention to detail—along with hundreds of brass nails—go into luggage pieces made by Louis Vuitton, above. Dining at the Vuitton mansion includes dinnerware graced with the company's signature initials, right.

REDISCOVERING THE PAST

*L*ace blooms beneath her hands like a snow-white flower, but ever so slowly. When Mylène Salvador works on her commissions, hundreds of hours are spent pinning and weaving the patterns that lace-making requires. Almost a lost art, such labor is the work of her heart. One hundred fifty years ago, more than 5,000 lace makers worked in Normandy twirling their bobbins.

Mylène wanted to make her own—only to learn that all directions had vanished with the years. She was drawn to these antique laces, she says, "because of their beauty, of course, but also by the intelligence, the logic, even the mathematics behind the patterns. They were as intriguing to me as the game of chess." She spent endless hours analyzing them until she deciphered the patterns and techniques. Now those who want to learn come to her École de la Dentellerie in Bayeux, where they are taught the techniques that she rediscovered.

At Château de Baccarat, above, the sparkle and gleam of fine crystal is everywhere, part of the two-hundred-year tradition of the firm. In the dining room, right, Baccarat crystal holds pride of place in the newly refurbished room, where the eighteenth-century paneling has been painted in pale celadon.

bags and trunks, silver-topped jars for makeup and powders, cases that folded out into beds. Such pieces were—and are—crafted with the same care as fine furniture to withstand the bumps of steamship and carriage. Now that people travel lighter, these firms have become famous for magnificent leather goods and other accoutrements of daily living, all crafted with similar care. The collections of the these makers of fine goods are historic trea-sures as well as design resources for modern creations. At Hermès, for instance, old bridles and saddlery are a mine of design inspiration for silk ties and handbag fittings.

Today such craftspeople are often concentrated in towns long known for their devotion to creativity and crafts-manship: Limoges is synonymous with fine porcelain, Quimper with pottery, Lyons with silk, and Alsace with wall-papers and cloth. France, and the world, are full of people who will be satisfied with only the best, the prod-ucts of those who work slowly, carefully, and proudly.

Exceptional wallpapers from the Zuber factory in Rixheim in Alsace have been the connoisseur's choice since the eighteenth century, when wallpapers enjoyed their first flowering. These are papers of particular art and charm: Completely handmade, they are lush and lavish, with textures and colors that only hand-brushed paints and hand-carved printing blocks can yield.

Ledgers containing samples of papers made over the course of two hundred years—many of

L U X U R Y   W A L L P A P E R

which are still in production—line the shelves of the old factory, and the printing blocks are arranged nearby. Fashion's changes can be traced in the company's designs, from the faux silks and festoons to the neo-Gothic patterns so loved in the nineteenth-century. But Zuber's finest glory has always been the panoramic papers that wrap a room in one continuous scene from doorway to windows, often picturing an exotic location—or a French artist's image of one. Some of the most popular are the designs that depict America in the 1830s, when Europe's love affair with the scope and grandeur of this country began in earnest: winding views of New York harbor, a veritable forest of ship masts, and a noble view of the banks of the Hudson River.

The showroom is in the firm's original factory, a graceful old building covered in vines, above. Within, rich and rare papers are on display, including neo-Gothic borders, left, for visitors to marvel at.

Zuber papers are still made in the traditional way—on long tables, where lengths of plain heavy paper are brushed with a background color before large wooden printing blocks, composed of several layers of wood, are inked and placed on the paper with pressure applied by a lever. Made by skilled carvers, the blocks can date back hundreds of years; more than a thousand of them are required to produce the company's most complicated designs. The result is a marvel, and collectible even in its smallest snippet.

The fountain plays in the factory courtyard, below left, while upstairs under the broad old beams, above left, printing blocks await the next order. Sheets of wallpaper are hung to dry completely between each layer of printing, opposite.

GARDENS

ne of the glories of France is the garden—whether a regal and formal creation, rigorously designed and meant for promenading, or the tangle of roses, herbs, and hortensia that is a cottager's pride. French gardens mirror the country's history and love of beauty. In the seventeenth century, kings and nobles built their palaces surrounded by a precise geometry of gardens that reflected both their control of the country and man's

The Bagatelle in Paris's Bois de Boulogne boasts more than 700 varieties of roses.

presumed hegemony over nature. Designers like Le Nôtre—who planned Versailles' allées, parterres, and jetting fountains, with an axis of pathways that intersected broad green lawns and marching boxes—created a pattern copied around the world. Just a hundred years later, a more romantic taste led to less disciplined beauties, with ruins, fountains, statues, flowing vines, and flowers offering a more poetic view of nature.

France's public gardens preserve some of the royal fancies for our enjoyment; many of Paris's most beautiful public parks, in fact, have royal roots. The tidy green lawns and neoclassical urns overflowing with flowers in the Luxembourg Gardens surround the palace where Marie de Médicis could watch the fountains play from her balcony. In the Bois de Boulogne, a pleasure ground since the seventeenth century, is the Parc de Bagatelle, created by a count who wagered Marie Antoinette that he could build an estate in just weeks. It flowers still with a symphony of roses, wisteria, daisies, and jonquils.

The Luxembourg Gardens are a traditional children's treat in Paris, where graveled paths make a satisfying crunch under flying feet, dozens of cupids pose ready for the counting, and face-painting delights the youngest of visitors.

VERSAILLES

Life at Versailles had all the beauty of a music box, a march of formal duties that engaged the entire court. Etiquette ruled, with the king and queen immured within the machinery, progressing through their ceremonies from morning to night. It's little wonder that Marie Antoinette, bored and looking for new amusement, might want a retreat from the rigors of court life. But when she ordered Le Hameau—The Hamlet, a fairy-tale version of a country village—to be built in a corner of Versailles's vast park, she was responding to changing tastes in landscape design as well. The desire for more informal gardens, prompted by Gothic garden design in England and the return-to-nature philosophy of Jean Jacques Rousseau, had penetrated France. The queen played the farm girl in the most refined of ways, wearing a simple linen dress and carrying a silver milk pail. At The Hamlet, the sheep were perfumed, the roses meticulously trimmed, the cows kept in barns built beside a lily-lavished lake. Today the retreat has been re-created under the trees of Versailles, and the gardens are tended as if their royal mistress was just a step away.

CHAMPAGNE

his is the wine of celebration—golden, effervescent and synonymous with joy. The very sound of the cork's loud pop summons high spirits, and for hundreds of years a small area around Reims in Épernay in northeastern France has been the best source of this elegant elixir. All wines are the sum of weather and soil, grapes and knowledge, but to be properly called Champagne, a bottle must be filled with the juice of the

Each bottle is turned daily as it matures; a candle is still used to inspect the contents.

grapes grown in the chalky soil found in this area and treated to cellar methods that have not changed in hundreds of years.

Champagne's origins date back to the seventeenth century, when certain wines failed to develop properly in the traditional casks. Vintners throughout the area tried bottling the grape's juice directly, and discovered that it became naturally sparkling. (A monk, Dom Pérignon, is credited by some with "inventing" this new wine, though history isn't certain.) The rarity soon was a favorite at the English and French courts, and wine growers like Claude Moët, Philippe Clicquot, and Perrier-Jouët traveled the world supplying the finest cellars.

Their descendants preserve the techniques that time has taught them. Champagne still requires close attention and a ritualistic regard for technique. Bottles need many months in the cellars, where they are inspected by candlelight and carefully rotated by hand an eighth of a turn each day, until they mature, producing the alchemy that results in a drink that seems a cascade of stars.

The advance of time, let alone technology, seems to have been roundly ignorged by Champagne vintners. Romantic nods to the wine's pioneers, above and below, testify to the enduring gratitude of all who enjoy Champagne.

ROMANCE

'AMOUR—THE VERY WORD HANGS IN THE AIR LIKE A SIGH. AN OLD GENTLEMAN TIPS HIS HAT TO HIS LONG-AGO LOVE, AND THE HEART TAKES WING. THIS IS A COUNTRY WHERE LOVE'S LABORS ARE NEVER LOST, AS GENERATIONS TEND THE ROSES THAT TWINE AROUND ANCIENT WALLS, PERFUME MAKERS DISTILL THE SUMMER'S BLOSSOMS, AND THE POETRY OF LOVE AND LIFE TRANSCENDS THE DAY.

FRAGRANCES

he rose unfurls like romance itself, from

the bud tight with promise to the full-blown beauty

that dances on the breeze. Each summer, the air is

filled with the scent of the flowers that launched a

thousand loves. In the south of France, the flowers

that tint the hillsides in a watery wash of color and

fill the breeze with fragrance are the very stuff of

romance—or at least of the perfumes that fuel it.

Perfumer Jean-Paul Guerlain finds inspiration in his family's lavish gardens.

only her scent behind. Jasmine and linden blossom, heliotrope and carnation, in blends known only to the perfumers, fuel our dreams and light our memories. And the rose's eternal power has its own enchantment, the sweet fragrance a reminder of a handful of buds that marked a special day.

Once such a pleasure was the preserve of the rich and powerful. It was Catherine de Médicis who, when she arrived in France as a royal bride in the sixteenth century, and longing for the fragrances she knew in Italy, ordered scented liquids and creams to be sent to her. Soon the sunny hillsides outside Grasse were planted with blooms to imitate them. Louis XIV was so enamored of perfumes that he ordered all members of his court to wear a new fragrance each day, and walked his gilded halls surrounded by the attars and elixirs used to scent a glove or a handkerchief.

Though they began as an aristocratic entitlement, restricted to use by the land's nobility, perfumes soon became a daily delight for everyone— a necessity, in fact, in an age that thought fragrances could ward off

The flowers that grow so abundantly in the south of France are carefully gathered, opposite, and distilled into perfume, then preserved in bottles like these from the nineteenth century, above, embellished with a fine detailing of filigree and hand-painted stoppers.

For hundreds of years, this land so full of light and long summer days has been the place where alchemy transforms the flowers' perfumes into sparkling bottles on the dressing table, elixirs so powerful that with just a whiff we're whisked away to an evening in our childhood, when Mother bent low for an evening kiss before dashing off to a party, leaving

CELEBRATING THE LINDEN

*I*n late spring in this Provençal valley, when the sun shines strong, the trees blossom, and all the world is green, the lindens flood the air with the aroma of honey and vanilla. The landscape is rough, abrupt, with stony hilltops carving the sky, but here in the town of Buis-le-Baronnies, the graceful linden trees, 30,000 of them, that have grown from seeds planted nearly two hundred years ago crowd about. In the farmhouses of the valley, the bustle begins as villagers search the barns' lofts for the ladders and the sacks that await this yearly ritual, when the linden trees yield their blossoms. Up the harvesters go, carefully plucking each flower, then bringing them all home to dry in

the attic lofts. By July the flowers are ready to be sold to those who want the linden for tea, perfumes, or lotions. The farmers gather up large jute squares to be filled with blossoms until they burst from the top, as the bags are piled in large mounds near the river. Buyers rub a petal, sniff the fragrance, and dicker over the price. Then, when all the flowers are sold, Fair Day begins in a village decorated with ribbons and linden wreaths, as everyone feasts and drinks large cups of iced tea made of linden, cassis syrup, sugar, and lemon, rejoicing in the wish, "Let the linden tree grow forever."

disease, lift a mood, or cure an illness, as well as add a grace note to the everyday. Soon families of perfumers around Grasse began to refine and experiment with the bounty of blossom that lay about them. The grand "noses," like Monsieur Guerlain, who was trained by his grandfather to recognize hundreds of scents, blend their choices from the flower fields—a bit of tuberose, some bergamot, perhaps a soupçon of *muguet de bois*—to create something entirely new. Such treasured formulas are secret, passed like gold to the next generation.

Each era has its own favorites. The Victorians collected beautiful bottles

The delicate sweetness of the lily of the valley, above, is celebrated each May Day, when flower sellers throughout Paris offer small bouquets to pin on lapels. Lavender, left, never fails to evoke hot summer days in the sun.

and filled them with fragrances compounded of Parma violets, perhaps, or Guerlain's 'L'Heure Bleue.' Men might come home from the barber in clouds of lime blossom, and by the beginning of this century, the great couturiers knew their customers not only by the cut of their dresses but by the colognes and perfumes they wore.

Not a great deal has changed in the way fragrances are compounded. Fields spring into bloom, and the blossoms are harvested by hand; such a tender treasure cannot be squandered or damaged as it's gathered. In small factories dotted around Grasse, the old ways are preserved as the flowers are distilled, then mixed with alcohol and poured into bottles that speak of the treasure within, often a triumph of the glass-blower or metalworker's art.

Today we bring French flowers into our homes in so many ways— in potpourri, candles, or an oil, in a cream for the skin or a splash of cologne. Such perfumes are the sum of sun and scent, one of France's great gifts to the world.

For more than sixty years, the gardens of Château de Canon in Calvados, opposite, have been tended by Marie-Antoinette de Carpentier. Her family's inheritance includes a beckoning series of walled gardens that lead from phlox to pinks to roses.

A FAMILY OF PERFUMERS

In Provence there is always a flower waiting to be picked," says Agnès Costa. All through the childhood she shared with sister Françoise, flowers framed their sunstruck days. Around them grew lavish blossoms to be gathered for a sweet-smelling bouquet on their way home from school, or stalks of lavender to crush in their hands in order to catch their scent in the air. They often visited the family's perfume factory in Grasse, which produced the well-regarded Fragonard fragrances, to watch the flowers bloom anew as scents to be poured into the beautiful bottles, like the one at right, that marched along the fac-

tory line. When they graduated from college, their father asked them to join the firm to bring new ideas to the old fragrance house; ten years later, the sisters still work happily together. "Françoise likes to have a steady, quiet life in the countryside, and I love to talk and travel," says Agnès, "so she stays home and takes care of the day-to-day operations while I promote the company around the world."

A bright Provençal sun has been added to the Fragonard packaging, and new scents and fragrances are being created. Their mother, Hélène, is the latest member of this family project: Her love of exquisite fabrics and her appreciation of the past led her to open a museum in Grasse dedicated to

regional costumes and jewelry, with a gift shop full of treasures for visitors to purchase. Included in her displays are laces as delicate as seafoam on a Provençal dress, above, and antique jewelry, left. Her collection also serves as inspiration for a home textile line that she has begun producing. This is one family that truly speaks for the time-honored ways of this corner of France.

Wandering among the roses at La Roseraie du Val-de-Marne, in the small town of L'Haÿ-les-Roses not far from Paris, is almost like watching fireworks—scarlet cascades high overhead, then a fountain of pink blossoms surges nearby. Yellow buds beckon visitors forward, and crimson blooms fill the background. The display is dazzling, a collection of sweet fragrances founded entirely on one man's love for one flower. More than a hundred years old, this is the most spectacular garden

LA ROSERAIE DE L'HAŸ

The formality of a classic French garden has been lavished with the fleeting beauty of thousands of roses. Each step reveals a changing vista of formality softened by tousled petals and bright green leaves.

to celebrate just the rose, in all its infinite varieties, from hybrids to Gallicas, tea roses, and blowsy moss roses.

Perhaps, as with many loves, Jules Gravereaux had no idea his heart would be consumed by the rosebushes that were scattered about the country estate he bought in 1892 when he left Paris. Only one year later he began buying roses in great quantities, amassing crates of new plants, writing to other passionate collectors about roses for cuttings, and keeping his gardeners busy tucking the new plants in their beds. In 1899 he asked famed landscape architect Edouard André to design this garden full of graceful arches and stone walls. Nearly 4,000 varieties came to be planted here. They are arranged on an

LA MARSEILLAISE

1976

DELBARD

axis of graveled paths that illustrate, in the most charming way, the evolution of the rose, from shy, wild varieties to long-legged and colorful hybrids. Any pedagoguery is lost on the visitor who yields to the temptation just to wander when the sky is full of flitting birds and flowering roses fill the view. For a century, the artful profusion has drawn visitors like Isadora Duncan, who danced among the blooms, and the poet Gabriele D'Annunzio, who proclaimed, "You must have excess in love!" Gravereaux's love of the rose gave meaning to his life, and gives joy today to those who come to see the bounty he left behind.

The roses that wind their way along the promenade of the stately Roseraie de Madame, below, are premier varieties selected for cutting, such as 'Jacques Esterel' and 'Grandmère Jenny.' Precise labels, opposite and above, let visitors take home ideas as well as memories.

F L O W E R S

o village is without one, nor any Paris street—the flower shop on the corner where a bouquet is as easy to find as a loaf of bread, and nearly as indispensable. Flowers of all sorts—a brilliant window box display or a handful of tulips in a pitcher—are a daily pleasure for the French, a glorious necessity. Some flower vendors, however, know there's no match for the rose, in all its varieties and shades. Some shops and their offerings

Roses for the picking can be found almost anywhere in France.

may be humble, relying on seasonal blooms for those who come to buy; others, like Lachaume in Paris, which has been dressing the rue Royale for a hundred and fifty years, prompt passersby to stop, look, and catch their breath at the imaginative displays within. There are endless variations for the flower seller who knows what he loves. Pascal Debrée loves only white flowers, and fills his Paris shop, Camélia blanc, with white blossoms grand and simple, from snowball hydrangeas to Queen Anne's lace, feverfew, and, of course, the rose, in arrangements that are a unique combination of sophistication and artless charm.

At Marianne Robic's shop in Paris's 7th arrondissement, her love of the rose sparks her bouquets. For Valentine's Day, it's no surprise that she pairs roses with glossy green foliage, but her roses also find a mate in tiny purple violets, like a sprinkling of petals from a medieval tapestry. At D. Rose, owner Dani has furnished her simple shop with a rose to suit every mood and containers that range from earthenware jars to sparkling glass vases. "Parisians love these flowers,"

Even the simplest presentation techniques attract patrons' eyes. A plain pitcher sets off a 'Magic' at D. Rose above, while 'Blue Belle' roses tucked in a ribbon beneath a scroll of paper, opposite, are the picture of perfection.

A PAINTER'S VILLAGE

At twilight on a June evening, the lanes of the small village of Gerberoy in Normandy fill with townspeople drawn outdoors by the sweet scent of the roses that grace nearly every street corner. Here, as the sun sets and the wind stirs the leaves, a quiet beauty lives on in this sleepy town—a beauty captured in the paintings of the French Impressionist Henri Le Sidanier, who

went to Gerberoy in 1901 and made the gentle beauty his subject. He worked for years on the grounds of his cottage, above, to create vest-pocket gardens, including a roseraie, that filled his hopes—and his canvases. He gave many of his neighbors plants, which have grown to spread an enchantment of roses by the small Norman cottages. Each year, in the Fête des Roses, villagers remember the painter who cast his colors over their village forever.

she says, "and they don't wait for special occasions to buy them." Some customers come once a week for a dozen or so; others come every day for one perfect stem. She allows the beauty or the flower to speak for itself by filling her tiny shop, with spare wooden tables, antique mirrors, and old tools on the walls for decoration. She wraps her flowers simply, in plain white shopkeeper's paper, and ties an extra 'Blue Belle' rose to the packet along with a scroll of paper for a message. And there is no doubt what the Left Bank shop Au Nom de la Rose proffers. Owner Georges Barthes orders his flowers from Provençal greenhouses year-round. He searches for the old-fashioned roses that prompt visitors to bury their noses in the petals in pursuit of their evocative scent. He is convinced we are all looking for "subtle perfumes in the gardens of our youth," and believes that the rose has an emotive power beyond other flowers. "Through our designs, we share our memories and dreams with our customers," he explains. "These are the roses of yesterday and always."

Only white flowers are sold in Paris's Camélia blanc in shades from cream to snow and in endless varieties, including the viburnum, left. Owner Pascal Debrée uses white roses, of course, but also favors stock, calla lilies, and snowball hydrangeas.

In a city that spreads the splendor of flowers throughout its streets, whether in public gardens or private windowsills spilling over with blooms, where no table is complete without its own bouquet and nosegays dazzle a hostess or delight a lover—in such a place, the bouquets wrought by Parisian Christian Tortu are something special. He is a man who celebrates flowers in all their permutations and possibilities, a poet of posies who has never seen a stem

MAÎTRE DE BOUQUETS

Roses are one of many flowers born to blush in a bouquet created by Christian Tortu, above. Sweet peas, bachelor's buttons, and pansies mingle with tender pink roses, opposite.

he didn't like or couldn't find a use for. At his shop, Carrefour de l'Odéon, clients and browsers circle the room, bending low to smell the fragrances, marveling here at a rose variety never yet seen in Paris, touching there a trembling leaf that adds a bold note of green to a handful of pink buds. Simple containers and unusual juxtapositions of texture and tone are part of his art—see how a simple metal mesh vase sets off a bounty of roses that ring changes from blush to bold to small clusters pink as a baby's fist. Christian is also known for using foliage in ways that complement the flowers, circling a bouquet with leaves like a collar to best show them off. He is known for his clever combinations and use of materials: Why not send roses floating among votive candles in a bowl, or

surround them with red berries, or tie them with raffia for a nosegay? As beautiful as these flowers are to the eye, visitors also savor the fragrances throughout the shop, especially at a counter with herbs that lend their own distinction to the air.

For Christian, gathering the bounty of field and flower is at the center of the beauty he creates. "I attended the École de Floriculture, where I learned a great deal. But the best advice on flowers came from my mother and my grandmother as we took walks through the Loire countryside. Their advice: 'Treasure them all.' " Today his search takes him to fields where humble Queen Anne's lace can be snipped to partner the elegant ivory 'Bianca' rose, like a parade of clouds, and pink onion flowers wait to counterpoint the coral of a bunch of antique roses. Berries are joined with crimson 'Extase' roses, seed pods stand bobbing their heads in a galvanized bucket, and great stalks of anthurium, olive, and magnolia leaves wait to frame fine flowers nearby. "There are no unlovely flowers in nature," Christian says firmly, as he reaches for some humble field poppies.

A large staff at Carrefour de l'Odéon is needed to fill the shop's many orders, below. Bouquets combining flowers of similar hues of dissimilar flowers, such as sunflowers and yellow-lined chartreuse roses, make noesgays that are sophisticated yet full of charm.

C O L E T T E

er eyes, wide as a child's, regard the world with a measuring glance, taking in all there is to see. "Look for a long time at what pleases you, and longer still at what pains you," Colette once said. Her art was found at the point where wisdom and pleasure meet, filled with sharp humor and a taste for life's joys, and melded with supple language and strong characters. Colette gave us romance, a wordly look at a vanished time and vanished places,

Colette captures her childhood home in Burgundy in her book My Mother's House.

Saint-Sauveur-en-Puisaye never faded. It was "a house that smiled only on its garden side," she once wrote, and she knew—and wrote of—every inch of that house and that garden, from the smell of tomato leaves in July to the twin firs in the upper garden to the lavender wisteria blossoms in spring. "With what might and main did I cling to you, and how afraid I was, even then, of losing you! I trembled at the mere thought of the more ruthless and less rare ecstasy of love!" she wrote of her childhood home. She was a favorite within her family—she was the baby, and everyone was enchanted with her blue eyes and golden hair, shampooed in rum and egg yolk. It was her character, though, that was her truly unique quality; a teacher once wrote that she was "imaginative, but one senses a stubborn determination to set herself apart." Her dream world came to an abrupt end when she was seventeen. The family, bankrupt, was forced to leave their house forever.

Her marriage in 1893 to Henri Gauthier-Villiers lasted for too many years: "Willy" took her writings and published them under his own name

"O solitude of my young days! You were my refuge, my panacea, the citadel of my youthful pride," Colette *recalled, dreaming of days when the fields were full of flowers, the wisteria twining about the old stone.*

suffused with recollections of a childhood full of the joys of family and countryside and a later life that knew pain as well as pleasure. In novels, essays, and, above all, in her autobiographical sketches, Colette is clear about what lies at the very heart of life.

Born Sidonie Gabrielle Colette in Burgundy in 1873, she had a well-furnished childhood, one that she drew upon her entire life, for memories of her loving mother and the house in

MUSÉE COLETTE

The farmhouse in Saint-Sauveur-en-Puisaye that Colette loved so remains a family's home, but much of her life is celebrated and re-created in a new museum in the local castle, which dominates the village where she was born. Here the very walls speak of her, as recordings of her voice reading favorite passages echo in the hall while visitors wander among displays of her manuscripts, her pens, and her eyeglasses, then pause in the café for a sampling of the hot chocolate she so adored.

Some of her furniture is used within the museum to re-create her Paris apartment in the Palais-Royal, the walls lined with thousands of photographs that capture her very public life after she became well-known and moved in literary and social circles. In the bedroom, left, is the bed where she spent so many hours writing with a blue paper lampshade to temper the light. Those passing at night could glimpse the blue light and know she was hard at work within. Many of the precious paperweights she collected, above, glow like jewels in the vitrine nearby. Such riches came to her late in life, but it was the winding village street and the stone house that gave her her real riches—those of memory.

to great acclaim. (The Claudine novels —semi-autobiographical creations that drew on her childhood memories— remain among France's most successful books of all time.) When she finally broke away, she discovered the joys of bohemian life in Paris, where she acted on the music-hall stage, flirted, fell in love, and wrote more books. It was there that she found her own voice—and a public that devoured her portraits of Belle Époque life and of women's search for love and respect. Her writing was filled with sensitive observations, evocative language, and great energy; she seems to have noticed everything, from her earliest childhood on, and her essays in particular drew such fine pictures of the past and present that readers felt they were a part of her experiences. With *Chéri*, *Gigi* (which appeared in 1945), and numerous essays, she secured a unique place for herself in this century's literary legacy. By the end of her life, she had become not only a model for young writers but a national treasure as well. In 1954 she became the first woman in France to be given a state funeral.

Leslie Caron, left, who played Gigi in the 1958 film of the same name, adores the Palais-Royal, Colette's home toward the end of her life. A menu for the Grand Véfour restaurant, designed by Jean Cocteau, above, is a reminder that this was her daily destination.

STYLE

HIC—EVEN THE WORD

IS FRENCH. FOR HUNDREDS OF YEARS,

THE WORLD HAS LOOKED TO

FRANCE FOR MATCHLESS LUXURY AND

STYLE. MASTERING THE ART

OF LIVING WELL IS A LESSON FROM

THE CRADLE, DELIVERED

FROM MOTHER TO DAUGHTER AND

TAUGHT BY EXAMPLE EVERY DAY,

UNTIL ELEGANCE SEEMS EFFORTLESS,

AND EVERYWHERE.

FASHION

ow do they do it? For hundreds

of years, the French have led the world in fashion, whether

in the great couture houses or on the streets, where

every woman seems to know just how to tie her scarf or set

her hat, even as the vagaries of style change by the

moment. Shoppers have been drawn to France since the

Middle Ages to buy all manner of luxuries and carry them

home, but not many of us manage to achieve that utterly

Designer Vanessa Bruno epitomizes the French talent for combining classics with flair.

French quality of insouciance, knowledge, and care that make a well-dressed Frenchwoman like no one else in the world. Even jeans somehow look different on these elegant, long-limbed bodies. Is it self-possession, even self-satisfaction? Perhaps—but that's undeniably part of the appeal.

There may well be vanity here, but it's of the right sort, a healthy pride that comes from thinking oneself worth lavishing attention upon. There is dedication to looking good at all times—no Frenchwoman would step out—even to the corner shop for milk—without checking the mirror first. She knows herself, and tempers the winds of fashion with her own selections. What she has is well chosen, bought after due consideration, and often from the shops she was introduced to by her mother and has visited all her life. She's likely to buy classics, then perhaps update them a bit as the times demand, because she knows things of quality will last forever if they're cared for.

Frenchwomen are born into this great heritage of fashion. Hundreds of years ago, one's position in society was announced by one's dress. The amount of lace one was allowed to wear—and even color choices—were decreed by the king's sumptuary laws. But the beautiful adornments were too irresistible to remain the jurisdiction of the court for too long, and

The Frenchwoman crafts her silhouette carefully, piece by piece, instinctively sensing when the scarf is just right, when a hat is needed. The same attention is directed to her shoes, hose, lingerie, and jewels.

With a beauty that has been adored for centuries, lace graces modern designs, as with these luxurious laces from Caudry, the traditional center for lace-making. Though most lace is now machine-made, conservators and the dedicated still resort to their needles or weave lace with bobbins to the old patterns so that they themselves may create authentic pieces.

eventually Paris and the provinces were filled with luxurious ribbons and laces, exquisite shoes, and woven silks. For generations, France has led the world in innovation in fashion—ladies of Boston who came to Paris to buy their gowns in the nineteenth century would store them unworn for a season or two, lest their forward thinking frighten the proper precincts at home.

Some things have changed since then—the great couture houses are not the all-powerful style setters they used to be, and their patrons and designers are often not even French. But the boutiques still hum, and Paris's grand department stores are never uncrowded. The survival of the luxury merchants, dressmakers, leatherworkers, and milliners who produce elegant clothing, shoes, and jewels is a testimony to the faithful French shopper. She knows her own style and has her own fashion sense. She is smart enough not to sacrifice her chic to the ephemeral, for she is well aware that true fashion lies beyond the day's enthusiasms, deep within her own heart.

THE FACE OF FRANCE

The look is inimitable and irresistible: From the youngest citizens to the oldest, the French carry on their faces what they themselves might call a certain *je ne sais quoi*—an appeal mysterious and individual. Part good health, part assurance, part vanity, French style extends beyond

clothing. Attention to detail is inherent. Impeccable grooming, a certain polish about face and hands contribute. The attitude is as natural as it can be, with "age appropriateness" at work everywhere: Here children carry their innocence, and adults their accomplishment, on their faces.

For hundreds of years, the little town of Romans, near Lyons, has had a rhythm of its own—the rushing of water from the mountainsides flowing through the tanneries, the slippery sound of needles through leather, and the percussion of hammers tapping out shoes. Still the center of the luxury shoe trade, Romans now houses the International Shoe Museum—Le Musée International de la Chaussure—full of treasures pointing to the ages when elegance continued right to the toe.

A GALLERY OF SHOES

A miniature, above, shows the wooden model that was once the pattern for a gentleman's boot, a form carved to order. Delicate as a breeze, the silken shoes, opposite, were made for dancing.

In the fourteenth century it was gloves, finely sewn, embroidered, and jeweled, that were the mark of the man or woman, and leather workers in Romans produced those of the finest quality. By the seventeenth century, they were making beautiful shoes for royalty as well. Louis XIV requested that his be raised on high heels and tinted red. His courtiers followed suit, but no one outside the royal circle was allowed to wear shoes of that design.

As kings rose and fell, heel height did, too. In Napoleon's time, when the fashions of ancient Greece and Rome influenced dress, men and women chose light leather shoes somewhat like ballet slippers, sometimes tied around the ankle with ribbons, delicate and delicious. In our own century, we've seen a

similar journey up and down, from the towering stilettos of the 1950s to today's occasionally more reasonable altitudes.

This is only a small piece of the history illustrated at the shoe museum, housed in a former convent with three hundred years of history of its own. Ten thousand objects and 4,000 years of design are charted, including many fine examples of the sumptuously decorated shoes made for the aristocracy and the bourgeoisie in the past three hundred years. (The poor tended to wear out their shoes, so few examples survive.) Today, many of France's finest designers—Yves St. Laurent and Paco Rabanne among them—still turn to the workers at Romans to have their shoes made with the same exquisite craftsmanship.

French shoemaker Roger Vivier decorated his shoes, opposite, with a twinkling of jewels. Fine Chinese silk wraps the towering heels, above right; antique clips dress up this solid black shoe, below right.

INTERIORS

hâteau or cottage, set in a broad green field or perched above a rolling sea, or perhaps in a high-ceilinged Belle Époque building on a cobblestoned Paris street— a home for the French is as personal an expression as a signature—and just as refined. These are not houses to which there is easy access. An invitation to someone's home is a true mark of intimacy; even entertaining friends often takes place in a restaurant. Such houses,

The interiors of a grand château are filled with light and serenity.

grand or ordinary, large or small, are treasures, holding fast family memories, illuminating family life, and done up in individual style.

Respect for the past runs through these homes. Some people are lucky enough to have stores of family furniture, fine china, and other objects to use again and again in each new generation. This can be the happiest combination, allowing fresh eyes to find new ways to use and display the time-cherished and traditional. Imagine a pair of Louis XVI or François I armchairs, some candlesticks dripping crystals, a miniature or two to hang beside the fireplace or poise on a table—and suddenly a house is established. Even those not so blessed might acquire a modern reproduction of traditional styles, and live happily— and perhaps more practically and comfortably—with their choices.

As in all matters French, regional tastes remain a strong influence. Provence, for instance, provides a vocabulary of design that is appreciated around the world; there's something about the ease and sunny charm of the south that finds favor

An old Provençal farmhouse has been refreshed thanks its owners' quest for simplicity. The toned-down palette of cream and blue in the kitchen/dining room, opposite, echoes the shutters, right, on the ancient stones.

VIGNETTES OF HOME

No one knows how the home reveals the heart better than Florine Asch, a Paris-based painter whose sketchbooks are filled with the details of life. "I often choose a small area of a room and really focus in on the individual objects—they are the key to the owner's personality," she says. In a brushstroke or two she captures the bronze bookends in a study or the pen on the desk—even the stamp on a letter's envelope. Her sketchbook is her constant companion, filled with her impressions of the life around her. As she works quickly—just ten minutes is enough for an ink sketch (she fills in with watercolor later)—she captures daily life in midflight. Her notebooks become a kind of diary of the everyday in the best sense of the word. People in all walks of life are eager to have their homes captured on paper; Florine often makes her paintings gifts to friends, who marvel at her eye for what fills their lives. "People think you have to go to exotic places to find inspiration for your work," she says, "but I always find the most fascinating subjects right at my fingertips."

everywhere—though transporting the colors and simple furniture to an urban setting, whether in New York or Paris, is a relatively new trend. It is the modern sensibility in search of a quieter, simpler way of life that has cast a fresh look at the traditional styles that now happily translate from country cottages to big cities. In turn, provincial craftsmen have always had a keen eye for paring down urban excesses and creating furniture that is very easy to live with, its shapely style adding a clear note of graphic appeal to any house.

The art of selection is well practiced in the home especially these days, as the French are returning to the relatively spare interiors that were typical two hundred years ago, when the masters of even the grandest château refrained from overdecorating its graceful rooms and owners of simpler homes contented themselves with less. Some of the most beautiful interiors include only what really speaks to those who live there. As always in France, personal taste and expression are more important than the dictates of others.

The natural charm of the countryside develops overs years of loving attention—and room for the surprises nature brings, like the shock of pink clematis against old wood and the roses that make their way across tiled roofs.

Perhaps the most winning way with toile is to wrap a room in it, below. The repeated charm came from carefully etched plates of copper that could be printed easily in monochrome, in black, green, red, or blue on a cream or white background. The resulting sheets were so large that they were traditionally hung out the window to dry in the sunlight, right.

The result of so much taste and style is a worldwide love of the classics of French interior design. An enduring example is toile, that descendant of copperplate printed pattern on cotton that originated in the town of Jouy in the eighteenth century, with its endearing depictions of country life, events of the day, and court scenes. One of the most famous toile scenes, "The Balloon of Gonesse," playfully illustrates galloping horses and children climbing trees for the best view of the hot air balloon. Another classic is the cheery Provençal prints that were used everywhere in the south—from curtains to upholstery to aprons—often with a characteristic paisley-like motif.

French brides still aspire to setting up house with glittering crystal, handsome gilded mirrors, tableware and china from Quimper and Sèvres, and luxuries from Limoges. Tapestries have their place as well, along with the seemingly endless variety of objets d'art and bibelots that have been collectors' dreams for years—boxes, picture frames, and china ornaments, each marked with typical French wit—

MARK OF DISTINCTION

One of the most beautiful aspects of vintage linen is monogramming, that sinuous interweaving of stitchery that becomes the last trace of the owner, immortalizing the object with initials or even a full name. Once monograms were purely practical, a means of distinguishing ownership when linens for table, bed, and wardrobe were all white. Soon necessity was transformed into aesthetics, and monogramming became another way to show off the taste and style of the owner.

Today, the Paris-based fine linen company D. Porthault has become famous worldwide for its inspired monogramming, which began in the 1920s when Madeleine Porthault started creating extraordinary designs for her exclusive clientele. Royals and the rich commissioned one-of-a-kind pieces, like the pale pink interlocking L's made for Queen Liliane of Belgium in the 1930s. The company's *chiffres*—the sketches on translucent tissue that the embroiderers followed—are a treasury of the tastes of generations.

DREAM QUILTERS

*I*n nearly every proud Provençal girl's wedding trousseau there always lay a precious quilt or two. The all-white *boutis* is the classic bridal quilt, a triumph of fine needlework—and now the collector's joy as well. When Florence Maeght was growing up, these beautiful quilts were all about her, a favorite of local villagers as well as of her own grandmother. Passionate about needlework, Florence taught herself to sew and began making her own quilts. As an adult she moved to Paris, where she opened the charming shop Le Rideau, below, on

the Left Bank, where all manner of Provençal quilts can be had, along with antique linens and cheerful prints she designs herself. "Each quilt tells a story," she says of those that are still handmade by the women of Provence, each stitch carefully placed in much the same ways as generations of women have always embroidered their dreams.

monkeys holding candlesticks, for instance—and attention to detail.

Linens have also long attracted the world's desires, and embroidered tablecloths and fine bed linens make for a trousseau worth acquiring; today's collectors look again to the ravishing laces and linens of the last century, finding that even the plain woven linen sheets of a hundred years ago make the perfect curtain, slip-cover for a chair, or bed covering.

Making choices based on quality and perfection of detail is the hall-mark of French interior design. Enter a home in France and marvel at the hundred-year-old chair, the painted porcelain miniature, the length of toile at the window. Marvel at glorious French style.

The stitching is tiny, the effect sublime in these blue and white quilts, right, from Blanc d'Ivoire, a Paris shop. Every bit of quilt is precious, and smaller pieces will be stitched into pillowcases, lap rugs, a baby's blanket, or even a pincushion.

There is an island off the coast of Brittany where the ocean is moody and the sky is often full of clouds—until the wind blows. Then all becomes a symphony of crisp blue and white, sharp with the scent of the ocean. A popular refuge for Parisians in search of an antidote to city life, this is the Île de Ré, where life is unhurried and no one is ever too busy to be polite.

Gérard and Nicole Foumerie fashioned their own private refuge from a hodgepodge of

INSPIRED BY THE SEA

Nothing could be simpler than a beach chair in a courtyard beckoning a reader, opposite, and wildflowers massed in a random collection of old vases march down the stairs, above, to create a warm and welcoming atmosphere by the sea.

little eighteenth-century cottages and an old stable, assembling a home united by clean, clear spaces and bathed in light from the sea. Traditional terracotta tiled floors and plain white plastered walls offer a clean backdrop to the furnishings as well as a soothing environment for family living. "It's only a little house in a little village, but it has meant so much to us for twenty years," says Gérard. Making do has been the Foumerie family motto in this country home. Gérard delights in refurbishing old furniture or other finds, however improbable, and using them in the house—two old luggage racks serving as a coffee table in one of the rooms are a prime example. Sometimes just a lick of paint is all that's required, like bright blue splashed on a

sideboard. With the beautiful light shining in, unfussy curtains are called for, and drawn only at night. Flowers are all around, there for the gathering. There is a greenmarket just a step away, and the ocean not much more than that, with boats in the harbor ready for a day of sailing. In the house, in keeping with local tradition, are twining wreaths of sea lavender, said to bring good luck to the islanders who live there. The Foumeries think it's working perfectly.

In a modest house by the sea, the blue and white of water and sky are reflected in the same palette used for fabrics and paint. The informal furniture, throw rugs, and bare tile and wood floors make upkeep easy.

ANTIQUES

n a country that cherishes its past and makes room for reminders of its glorious history, it's little wonder that household treasures often take pride of place in a home. Sometimes they are preserved in all their splendor, even if there's a crack in the vase or a tear in the tapestry covering the seat, but others, less precious, can be reused or recovered, and they live on in a new guise to delight another generation. Visit a friend and

Antiques dealer Pétrusse replicated the beauty of cashmere shawls to use at home.

In Burgundy, an artist's home is an artful accumulation of furniture and collections amassed from the local village attic sales, keenly pursued over the years.

find a family's history displayed—an oil painting over the fireplace depicting a moustached grandfather, a dresser laden with gilded boxes, or a tablecloth of vintage lace.

The French love of antiques can also be a matter of practicality—no region, no town is without its *marchés aux puces*, or flea markets, where all the incidentals of lives past are pored over and put on display. This is recycling with style, for the discerning eye can spot the perfect use for an old pot—wouldn't it hold geraniums?—or snap up a piece of furniture that, with a bit of paint or polish, will give a room distinction. Avid hunters never have enough; visit the markets in Paris on the weekends and you'll be part of a crowd lost in a curious meditative haze, prowling through dozens of objects and searching hundreds of stands. Carried home in triumph, such finds are evocative additions to any home, bringing with them not only the echo of past lives, but of the chase and the bargain of today. Perhaps it's today's flea market find that will become a family antique for the generations to follow.

PORTOBELLO IN PARIS

There are certain shops that set the heart thumping, with beautifully displayed objects from many places and times. Paris's Portobello Antiques is just such a shop, filled with cashmere shawls, English bamboo, trailing lace nightgowns, fine faïence—all brought on consignment to Catherine Remoissenet, who has a gift for seeing beauty in the most unlikely places. "Customers have taught

me how to love and appreciate many kinds of merchandise that were not specifically my taste to start with," she says. She does have one requirement, though—all items must date from the 1850s to 1910. Her displays are so charming that everything flies out the door. Part of the pleasure of the store, for shoppers and for Catherine, are the surprises that arrive each day; for many, the shop is a place to stop each week, have a chat—and perhaps take something home to begin its life anew.

S H O P P I N G

ue du Fabourg-St.-Honoré. Boulevard St.-Germain. Rue du Bac. The very names of these storied Parisian streets summon up the delights of shopping in France. This is another aspect of French life where necessity and pleasure overlap; there are hypermarkets, of course, acres of wine by the liter and beans by the kilo, dispensaries of the basics of life. But it is in the fine shops where the French display their flair, where commerce can

Wide windows beckon shoppers to browse in these Paris shops.

When American Corey Amara married and moved to Provence, she haunted the flea markets. Her fine eye has found beauty in the humblest objects, like an old vase turned into a lamp, above. In the kitchen, opposite, shelves hold an assortment of everyday items full of wit and color.

almost seem secondary, so beautiful are the interiors and the objects on display. The very word *boutique* is French; it calls to mind all those small, very individual repositories of chic that are a shopping mainstay in big cities and small towns, where the very distinctive styles of the owners, and often the desires of the clientele, are allowed full play. Good design is rarely forgotten in even the least expensive

item—go to a French "five and dime" like Monoprix and just look at how handsome the pots and pans are, or drop in a hardware store and see that even the hinges and doorknobs are well designed.

In finer shops, sometimes it's enough just to wander from one pretty thing to the next, the eye pausing for a closer look at this napkin, that candlestick, those plates, these scarves. The

LETTER PERFECT

Perhaps it is not surprising that in a country that so prizes the word, a fine Parisian stationer is in its fourth generation of creating the most desirable papers for those who know to seek out the best. At Stern, founded in 1830, the engraver's art is celebrated in time-honored ways. There are just a few workers left who can engrave by hand using a tiny hammer and a chisel the size of a needle. The results are miniature portraits of

perfection, each line of a family crest or a wedding invitation crisp and distinct. Nearly anything can be engraved or embossed, from a guest book to a monogram for an invitation, from a signet ring to buttons for staff uniforms. Ask to look at Stern's book of designs and marvel at the intertwining initials of the Victorians, the elegantly simple characters of Art Deco, and the whimsies of today, like a wedding invitation embossed with a twirling lizard. If the past is any indication, Stern will continue to mark life's passages with pen and print forever.

displays are so wonderful, often offering clever decorating ideas or even amusement—who would have thought to display those candles in a drift of pebbles from the sea, or to match those colors? Look at the wall filled with antiques and modern objects for sale in a small town: They may just be humble items from a country kitchen, but a pile of lemons brings out the buttery tone in a bowl; the jugs once used to store olives are reinvented with a twist of Victorian artificial berries twined around their fat curves; an old grape-picking basket is revealed as a triumph of sculpture, of line and curve when it's placed high on a shelf.

In a country where people tend to buy one item of great quality rather than lots of little lesser things, shops cater to this way of thinking. Of course there are frills and furbelows, bought for a flirtation with the trendy or the ultrafashionable, and these are likely to be inexpensive or temporary, to be tossed away when the mood passes. But for the really important commodities of life—china and crystal, wine and cheese—shopping is

In France, objects of humble origin can be cherished. An old farmhouse bed, for instance, boasts iron curves worthy of Matisse, and a quartet of twigs eloquently enclose a mirror, above. Even milk bottles and scrubbrushes bask with paper labels and cotton cords, left.

Charlotte Gaveau has paired her love of tea and fanciful hats in her her shop in St.-Rémy-de-Provence; many of the hats are of her own creation. Nearby, Marie Ricco bakes cakes and sells antiques in another "combination" shop, opposite.

serious, a dance between patron and proprietor until the perfect item in the perfect moment is achieved. Often the shopkeeper is as emotional and passionate as the shopper—the woman who sells handmade laces from Brittany because she loves their exquisite beauty; the man who bought the failing china factories of Quimper because he couldn't bear to let beauty die and worked around the clock to revive them; the breadmaker who stipulates only this flour, only that shape, and can't keep up with demand. These are purveyors of the promise of excellence.

AT TABLE

O EXPERIENCE FRENCH CUISINE

IS TO COME TO THE VERY

HEART OF THE COUNTRY,

FOR GOOD FOOD WELL SERVED IS

A NATIONAL PASSION, PART OF

THE ESSENCE OF THE FRENCH

IDENTITY. NOWHERE DO

PEOPLE LINGER OVER FOOD AND WINE

AS THEY DO IN FRANCE.

CUISINE

t's early, and the sunlight is just finding the shadows in the doorways as the shutters roll up, the doors open, and the café tables and rattan chairs are drawn onto the sidewalk. Waiters bustle about, filling baskets with croissants, while the rich scent of coffee fills the air. Down the street, on this market day, farmers are already building small pyramids of fruit, white peaches heavy with juice and grapes in jewel tones, while nearby

Fine, fresh French bread partners every meal, from soup to cheese.

artichokes, bright orange carrots, and mounds of zucchini tower along the aisles. There's banter between the stalls as shoppers begin to arrive. Empty baskets over their arms, they walk with the kind of concentration seen in a museum and consider carefully, hefting an apple here, sniffing a melon there. Into the baskets go the makings for the day's meals; then there are visits to the butcher, the cheese shop, and, finally, the boulangerie for some baguettes. Finally the shopper makes her way home, basket laden to the brim. At the restaurant in the center of town, the chef and his assistants have been at work for an hour or so, slicing carrots and celery into matchsticks, filling up the stockpot that simmers at the back of the stove, and whipping up the cream for the tarts, while the menu is lettered with daily specials inspired by what's fresh at the market. Later on, you'll see whole families out to dine, the small children, slender legs dangling from their chairs, adept with knife and fork, and working their way from soup to cheese along with the rest of the group.

When chef Jean-Pierre Philippe enters the kitchen of his family restaurant, La Toque Blanche in Les Mesneuls, he draws on impeccable local ingredients and memories of his mother cooking here. Such was the traditional preparation for his current status as one of France's leading chefs.

BAKED ONION SOUP

Serves 6 to 8

When the old market Les Halles was the source for food in Paris, purveyors and shoppers warmed themselves in the cold hours of the morning with a bowl of onion soup topped with melted cheese.

7 cups chicken broth

2 thyme sprigs

2 bay leaves

6 tablespoons (¾ stick) unsalted butter

2 tablespoons vegetable oil

3 garlic cloves, finely chopped

3 pounds white onions, thinly sliced

¾ teaspoon sugar

¾ teaspoon salt

¾ teaspoon freshly ground black pepper

⅓ cup all-purpose flour

1½ cups dry white wine

¼ cup Madeira

1¾ cups grated Gruyère

6 to 8 slices French bread, cut into 1-inch-thick slices and toasted

1. In a large saucepan, bring the chicken broth, thyme sprigs, and bay leaves to a boil. Remove from the heat. Cover and let stand.

2. In a heavy, large pot over medium heat, heat the butter and oil. Add the garlic and onions, stirring to coat. Cook for 45 to 55 minutes, stirring often, until the onions turn light golden brown.

3. Sprinkle the sugar, salt, pepper, and flour over the onions. Cook, stirring constantly, for 5 minutes.

4. Pour in the wine, stirring to scrape up any browned bits from the bottom of the pot. Stir in the hot stock and bring the soup to a boil. Reduce the heat and simmer for 30 minutes, stirring occasionally.

5. Remove the bay leaves and thyme sprigs. Stir in the Madeira.

6. Preheat the oven to 350°F.

7. Sprinkle a little Gruyère in the bottom of 6 to 8 ovenproof 20-ounce soup bowls. Arrange the bowls on a baking sheet.

8. Pour the hot soup into the bowls. Top each serving with a slice of French bread and the remaining Gruyère. Bake for 8 to 10 minutes, until the cheese is golden.

Could there be a finer afternoon than one spent at a charming hotel alongside a river in Burgundy, where white tablecloths echo the clouds that scud overhead and ducks peck anxiously for the last bit of baguette? This perfection is the work of one woman, Leslie Caron, who envisioned a hotel perched along the River Yonne near her home—and then possessed the wit and the will to create it.

"I used to cross the little bridge over

ROMANTIC RIVERSIDE INN

The medieval town of Villeneuve-sur-Yonne in Burgundy is Leslie Caron's home and the place where she has created an enchanting inn on the banks of the rambling river.

the river and see these old bricked-up warehouses lining the bank," she says, "and I thought they were charming." Their charm may have escaped most passersby, but Leslie had a vision, of the old stone repaired and glowing in the sun, of tall timbers dark with age, of the gleam of old furniture and bright fabrics—and of guests to enjoy them. "I never planned to be an innkeeper," she says now, but the project found her and caught her heart. Now, La Lucarne aux Chouettes—which she translates as "Owls' Lair"—is a reflection of the efforts, and the love, she has put into the transformation.

Simplicity and luxury are the bywords. Leslie trundled across the countryside, searching for old tiles for the floor, old mantlepieces for the fires,

armoires, beds, and chairs for every corner. "I even ordered the nails and cement," she says, and her glamorous film-star image recedes an inch or two. "Oh, this was much harder than making a movie," she explains with a laugh.

But slowly it all came together, from the toiles and laces in the bedrooms to the flowers gathered each day for the tables. Good food, too, was in her plans, so townspeople would come as well as visitors seeking a peaceful and pretty place to while away some days. Rare and wonderful wines are made nearby, and the chef turns out dishes that celebrate each season—a tomato baked with goat cheese or strawberries floating on cream.

Today the inn is a well-established favorite, both with travelers and Leslie's neighbors, who come in search of peace and plenty by the gentle riverside. Leslie is likely to be there, too, her eye on everything that makes the inn hum with the happy sound of those who came to the tiny Burgundian town and found a gentle paradise.

Leslie favored simple fabrics and furniture throughout the building, below. The old roof beams add a graphic note to many of the bedrooms, above, and an ancient fireplace warms the dining room, opposite.

STUFFED TOMATOES
À LA NIÇOISE

Makes 6 servings

Nice, in the hot dry south, is a center for olive growing. Groves of olive trees, with their silver green leaves, are planted across the hills. Preserved in brine, the fruit make their appearance in many dishes of the region, *à la Niçoise*.

6 tomatoes

CHEESE STUFFING:

5 ounces fresh goat cheese, such as Montrachet

¼ cup finely chopped red bell pepper

¼ cup finely chopped green bell pepper

1 tablespoon chopped chives

2 tablespoons heavy cream

Freshly ground black pepper, to taste

MUSHROOM SAUCE:

3 tablespoons unsalted butter

1 cup chopped fresh wild mushrooms

¼ cup chopped zucchini

1 cup chicken broth

1 tablespoon chopped fresh basil

Fresh dill sprigs, for garnish

1. In a large pot of boiling water, blanch the tomatoes until the skins loosen, 30 to 60 seconds. Remove the tomatoes from the water and carefully peel, spreading the skins out flat on paper towels for garnish.
2. Cut off the tops of the tomatoes and reserve. Using a spoon, scoop out the seeds and as much of the juicy inner flesh as possible, into a bowl, leaving a ¼- to ½-inch-thick shell.
3. Press the flesh and juice through a fine-meshed sieve; reserve the juice and discard pulp. Invert

the tomatoes onto a paper towel–lined plate to drain while preparing the stuffing.

TO MAKE THE CHEESE STUFFING:

1. In a medium bowl, combine the goat cheese, red pepper, green pepper, chives, cream, and pepper. Mix well and set aside.

TO MAKE THE MUSHROOM SAUCE:

1. In a medium-size skillet over medium-high heat, melt the butter. Sauté the mushrooms and zucchini about 2 minutes, until tender.
2. Stir in the chicken broth, basil, and reserved tomato juice. Bring the mixture to a boil. Remove from the heat and cover to keep warm.
3. Preheat the oven to 375°F. Spoon the cheese stuffing into the tomato shells. Top the tomatoes with the tomato "lids" and arrange in a 12- x 7½- x 2-inch baking dish. Pour the mushroom sauce around the tomatoes.
4. Bake for 10 to 15 minutes, until the stuffing is warm. Carefully remove from the oven.
5. Spoon the tomatoes and pan juices into shallow serving bowls. Garnish the tomatoes with dill sprigs and crumpled reserved tomato skins, if desired.

GRATIN DAUPHINOIS

Makes 6 to 8 servings

This dish, a specialty of the Dauphiné region, is substantial enough for supper, accompanied by a well-dressed green salad. For the long, slow cooking, choose a potato that will maintain its shape, such as a Russet.

3 garlic cloves, finely chopped

2½ cups heavy cream

2 pounds baking potatoes, peeled and thinly sliced, soaked in cold water

2 shallots, finely chopped

Salt and freshly ground white pepper, to taste

Freshly ground nutmeg, to taste

2 teaspoons dried thyme

2 eggs, beaten

¾ cup each grated Parmesan and Gruyère, mixed together

4 tablespoons (½ stick) unsalted butter, cut into bits

1. Preheat the oven to 350°F. Generously butter a 12- x 7½- x 2-inch baking dish and a piece of foil. Sprinkle the baking dish with the garlic to coat the bottom and sides of the pan.
2. In a medium-size saucepan, bring the cream to a boil. Remove from the heat and cover to keep warm.
3. Pat the potato slices dry on paper towels. In a large bowl, toss the potatoes with the shallots, salt, pepper, nutmeg, and thyme. Add the eggs and ½ cup of the cheese, mixing well to combine. Arrange even layers of the potato mixture in the prepared baking dish.
4. Pour the warm cream over the potatoes. Sprinkle with the remaining cheese and dot with the butter. Cover the dish with the prepared foil and place on a baking sheet.
5. Bake for 45 minutes. Remove the foil and bake for 30 to 45 minutes more, until the potatoes are tender. Let stand for 10 minutes before serving.

VARIETIES OF COOKING

It's certainly possible to eat badly in France, as it is anywhere else in the world, but ordinarily . . . who doesn't savor memories of dining brilliantly there? Consider a simple breakfast of café au lait and a croissant that breaks into buttery shards, or an omelette with frites and a glass of wine in a

bistro at noon, or a high-flying haute-cuisine evening prepared by a Michelin-starred chef with a gift for experimentation, or a dinner at home with beef bourguignon and a leafy green salad, and everyone lingering at the table deep in good conversation. Dining in France can be an eater's epiphany, a celebration of the marriage of fine ingredients and gifted cooks.

French cuisine has much to offer, varying by region, by degree of formality and ambition in the cook, and by history and taste. When, fifty years ago, the French gastronome Carmonsky wrote *La France Gastronomique—*

In every Parisian bistro, reliable pleasures are a familiar menu and a cozy informality that encourages guests to linger over each course of their meal.

and it took 32 volumes to cover the subject—he identified four distinct types of cookery: "la haute cuisine, la cuisine bourgeoise, la cuisine régionale, et la cuisine improvisée." The grand restaurants deliver haute cuisine, based on the classics of French cookery with their subtle saucing and luxury ingredients, with nouvelle cuisine being a 1980s quest by some chefs to lighten the tradition of rich and heavy preparations. Cuisine improvisée is the humblest of foods, the simple preparations of stews and omelettes that have filled farmhouse tables for generations. Cuisine bourgeoise is one of France's glories, the middle-class home cooking that requires an attentive cook, a good market, and Grandmother's recipes. Traditionally this was one of a wife's main duties, her day organized around the market visit and the careful preparation of food for her family,

Cheese speaks of its region
of origin. In Provence, chèvre,
made from goat's milk,
is a pungent partner to a
cuisine rich in vegetables.

PETITS SOUFFLÉS AU CHÈVRE

Makes 8 servings

The sharp taste of goat's cheese is splendid on its own and it can be the basis for succulent dishes like these little puffs. Watch carefully to prevent these from burning.

3 tablespoons unsalted butter
3 tablespoons all-purpose flour
1 cup milk, scalded
½ teaspoon salt
⅛ teaspoon cayenne pepper
2 ounces aged chèvre, grated or crumbled, plus 4 thin slices, for garnish
4 eggs

1. Preheat the oven to 400°F. Butter and lightly flour 8 6-ounce ramekins. Set aside.
2. In a medium-size saucepan over medium-low heat, melt the butter. Stir in the flour and cook, stirring, for 2 to 3 minutes. Slowly whisk in the scalded milk, whisking constantly, until the mixture thickens. Stir in the salt, cayenne pepper, and grated chèvre until the cheese melts. Remove from the heat.
3. Beat the eggs until very light and fluffy. Gradually whisk spoonfuls of the hot sauce into the beaten eggs. Whisk until smooth.
4. Set the prepared ramekins on a baking sheet. Pour ½ cup of the mixture into each ramekin. Bake for 18 to 20 minutes, until puffed and golden.
5. Using a heart-shaped cookie cutter, cut the chèvre slices into heart shapes. Remove the ramekins from the oven and serve at once garnished with the chèvre.

TREASURE HUNT

hen Bernard Loiseau feels the air dampen and chill in Saulieu, he may greet it with more joy than most. He is passionate about mushrooms, and knows all the ways to find them in the countryside. He was raised to search for this treasure. "Every Sunday, we would hunt for the cèpe mushrooms, then bring them home to dry," he says, remembering the delicate fragrance of the woods that came with them. Now, at his restaurant, La Côte d'Or, he shares his plunder with appreciative diners who know the rarity of what they savor, know how it is hunted so carefully and then carried

home in a basket that cradles them gently. Loiseau is happy when the nuance of the flavor adds its magic to a dish, during those few weeks when mushrooms are there for the gathering. "In order to cook for the present, you need to know the past, and to know how to cook well, you have to know how to eat well," he says, and the mushrooms he harvests are a part of the past he brings to share with his guests.

SAUTÉED FOIE GRAS WITH ROASTED CÈPES

Makes 4 servings

True luxury here—rich foie gras paired with lots of garlic and fragrant cèpe mushrooms. *Fleur de sel* is available at specialty food stores and has a light, smooth texture with a delicate taste.

    4 tablespoons goose fat or olive oil

    6 garlic cloves, sliced

    1¼ pounds cèpes, trimmed, rinsed, and patted dry

    Salt and freshly ground black pepper, to taste

    2 cups chicken broth

    2 tablespoons garlic purée or paste

    1 tablespoon minced fresh parsley

    8 slices of raw duck foie gras (about 2 ounces each)

    ***Fleur de sel*, if desired**

    Red wine vinegar, to taste

    1 tablespoon unsalted butter

1. Preheat the oven to 500°F. In a small skillet set over medium-high heat, heat 2 tablespoons of the goose fat. Add the garlic slices and cook until golden and crisp, 3 to 5 minutes. Remove the skillet from the heat and transfer the garlic to a paper towel–lined plate.

2. Cut the sides of the mushrooms to give them an oblong shape. Heat the remaining goose fat over medium-high heat. Add the mushrooms and salt and pepper, and cook, stirring occasionally, for 5 minutes, until the mushrooms are golden. Add 1 cup of the chicken broth and garlic purée, and reduce the mixture, stirring occasionally, by half. Stir in the garlic and parsley.

3. Season the foie gras with salt and pepper. Heat a nonstick skillet over medium-high heat, add the foie gras, and sear for 30 seconds on each side. Transfer the skillet to the oven and roast for 2 minutes. Remove the skillet from the oven and transfer the foie gras to a paper towel–lined plate. Sprinkle with *Fleur de sel*, if desired. Pour the fat from the skillet, add the vinegar and the remaining 1 cup of the chicken broth. Reduce the mixture over medium-high heat, stirring, by half. Swirl in the butter.

4. To serve, spoon the mushroom mixture onto four plates, top each with two slices of the foie gras, and drizzle with the sauce.

CLEMENTINE CRÈME BRÛLÉE

Make 6 servings

Crème brûlée, or "burnt cream," is actually a British invention, but the French have mastered the art of combining cream with sugar into a custard topped with crunchy caramel.

1 vanilla bean	3 egg yolks
3 clementines	½ cup granulated sugar
2⅓ cups crème fraîche	4 teaspoons crystallized
⅓ cup milk	sugar

1. Split the vanilla bean lengthwise and scrape the seeds into a small bowl. Zest one clementine, avoiding any white pith.
2. In a large saucepan over medium-high heat, combine the crème fraîche and milk. Add the vanilla seeds and clementine zest and bring to a boil. Remove the saucepan from the heat, cover, and let rest for 20 to 30 minutes.
3. Place the yolks and granulated sugar in the large bowl of an electric mixer. Using the whip attachment, mix for 5 minutes until the mixture lightens. Pour the cream mixture over the yolks and mix well. Refrigerate for 1 hour, covered.
4. Heat the oven to 300°F. Pour the cream into 6 6-ounce ramekins. Add the clementine quarters. Bake the ramekins for 30 minutes, until firm. Let cool on wire racks and powder the top with crystallized sugar. Heat the broiler and place the ramekins 4 inches from the heat source. Broil until the tops are golden, about 4 to 6 minutes. Cool the ramekins in the refrigerator for 2 to 3 hours until firm.

revelatory in flavor, reliable in its constancy. This sort of time-consuming cooking is under siege in France today as elsewhere, but serving the family home-cooked, delicious food is still a matter of pride for many. And it is the cuisine régionale that reflects the size—and the riches—of the country. Menus that reflect what can be found in a region are more than just a tradition—what would Brittany be without buckwheat-flour crêpes and seafood, or Normandy without apples and all that can be made from them, or Provence without that sunny cuisine of garlic and vegetables? What better expresses the weather, the land, the soil, of a place than the wine that comes from it, each bottle almost a diary of the days that passed in the growing season. Though some of these fine regional delicacies are exported—it's possible in Paris to dine on cuisine from around the country, as a restaurant ordinarily offers the food of its owner's native region— they're at their best on home ground, where the morels come from the forests nearby, the tomatoes are just plucked from the vines, the zucchini

blossoms freshly gathered. Sitting at such a table is a celebration of the earth, and the history, and of a place.

Still, there are certain constants throughout the country, certain elements of the meal that may be considered luxuries elsewhere but that in France are assumed and make the experience complete. Wine, of course—whether a drinkable red poured into a carafe at a café, a fine Champagne uncorked for a celebration, or something from the family cellar brought up to go with a stew—

Round and golden as the sun, the melons of summer are a partner to the digestif of melon liqueur that finishes an evening meal outdoors.

In Normandy, a flurry of blossoms in May heralds the apple, but it is a fixture on tables in the region all year, whether eaten from the hand, baked into a tart, or distilled into Calvados.

is always an accompaniment to dining. Cheese is another reliable source of pleasure: Visiting a cheese shop in Provence, for instance, where the selection may be laid out on leaves, prompts one of those long conversations, long considerations, and slivers to sample before a purchase is made. Charles De Gaulle famously complained of the difficulty of governing a country with 265 cheeses—and there are twice as many on the shelves now.

Finally, bread is more than the staff of life. The baguette is one of the symbols of France, though historians trace it to just a century ago, when it became the popular bread of Paris, bought twice a day so it was always fresh for both lunch and dinner, and a bit could be left over to be toasted for breakfast the next morning. But these days loaves are often made at central bakeries and suffer from mass production; the protection of the baguette in all its gold-crusted, crumbling perfection is a battle. Fine bakers who succeed will find a line around the block—visit Paris's Poilane early in the morning to see those who are passionate about their *pain* waiting for a loaf.

Only the Best

"Eat to live, not live to eat" is the perfectly expressed philosophy about dining. It's certainly one that preserves French figures for the fashions. If everything is of the best, then just a sliver will do to satisfy the appetite. Mothers cluck over their babies' plates, feeding them tiny portions of what their elders had for dinner. And ceremony is part of the enjoyment. Consider the cake: It's not a hunk of multicolored icings, but something to be chosen carefully at a pâtisserie

APPLE CHARLOTTE

Makes 6 to 8 servings

This traditional dessert celebrates the apples of Normandy— most grown there are cooking apples, and the region's cooks have invented endless ways to prepare the fruit.

10 Golden Delicious apples
¾ to 1 cup sugar
¼ cup Calvados, or to taste
8 to 10 slices brioche, cut about ¾-inch-thick
6 tablespoons (¾ stick) softened unsalted butter

1. Preheat the oven to 450°F. Butter a 9- x 13-inch baking dish.
2. Peel, halve, core, and slice the apples. Arrange the slices in the prepared baking dish and sprinkle with sugar to taste. Bake for 30 to 40 minutes, until soft. Remove from the oven and carefully add the Calvados. With a match, carefully flambé the apples. Reduce the oven temperature to 425°F.
3. Brush the bread slices with butter and arrange them on an ungreased baking sheet. Bake the bread for 5 to 7 minutes, until lightly golden brown.
4. Line a 6-cup charlotte mold or soufflé dish with parchment paper and butter the paper. Alternately layer the bread and apples in the dish. Put the mold in a baking pan and add enough hot water to the baking pan to reach halfway up the sides of the mold. Bake in the oven for 40 minutes. Cool and chill, covered, overnight.
5. To serve, run a thin knife around the inside of the mold. Invert the mold onto a serving dish..

MADELEINES

Makes 2 dozen

Marcel Proust and his madeleine are inseparable in our memories, but the little cake's origins lie long ago in the Lorraine. Just as a gala dinner was being prepared for a duke, the pastry maker stormed off in a huff. A young chambermaid offered to bake the cakes her grandmother had taught her to make, and when these were produced, the duke ordered they be named after her—Madeleine de Commercy.

3 eggs, plus 1 egg yolk
⅔ cup superfine sugar
2 tablespoons fresh lemon juice
1 teaspoon vanilla extract
Pinch of salt
1¼ cups sifted all-purpose flour
½ cup (1 stick) unsalted butter, melted
24 lemon balm leaves

1. Preheat the oven to 375°F. Spray 24 madeleine molds with a nonstick spray coating. Place the molds on a baking sheet.
2. In the small bowl of an electric mixer, beat the eggs and egg yolk with the sugar at high speed until pale and thick, about 5 minutes.
3. Beat in the lemon juice, vanilla, and salt. Using a rubber spatula, gradually fold in the flour until it is well mixed. Drizzle the butter over the batter and gently fold it in.
4. Cover the bowl with plastic wrap and refrigerate the batter for 30 minutes.
5. Spoon 1 tablespoon of the batter into each prepared mold. Do not spread the batter out. Top each mound of batter with a lemon balm leaf. Spoon 1 tablespoon batter over each leaf to cover completely.
6. Bake the madeleines for 20 to 25 minutes, until the edges are lightly browned and a cake tester inserted into the center of one madeleine comes out clean.
7. Carefully loosen the edges of the madeleines with a small knife. Invert them onto a wire rack to cool.

where the temptations are displayed like jewels in the cases, and just as well designed, well executed, and refined: lemon elevated into satiny, sunny tarts beautifully identified in elaborate chocolate scrolls as *citron*; sugar spun, then whirled over a creamy fantasy; a chocolate cake, say an *opéra*, that melds rich butter and dark chocolate into a glassy sculpture. Tucked into a stark white box, tied with a smart ribbon, this is not merely a cake; it

is an occasion, an event, to be eaten slowly, savored exquisitely, with observation, not greed.

DINING OUT

Such discriminating eaters also demand a wide variety of public places in which to make their repast. This is a social necessity too. An invitation to a French home is a rare thing, with family life a private preserve, so much of the enjoyment of fine dining comes in restaurants, for the French themselves as well as for visitors. There are many different types of eating places, to suit every mood, pocketbook, and occasion. The first restaurants date to the years after the Revolution, when chefs

Paris's famous pâtisserie Ladurée is a confectionery full of more temptations than can possibly be resisted, and a favorite place to buy the perfect macaroons in a palette of pastel hues, as chic as they are sweet.

THE BAKER'S DAUGHTERS

The fragrance floated through their childhood dreams. It was the scent of bread baking in wood-fired ovens, drifting up from their father's shop downstairs. For four generations, the Ganachaud family had risen at dawn, measured flour, kneaded the dough for loaves that are renowned in Paris. It seemed natural for daughters Isabelle and Valérie to follow in the floury footsteps. Schooling at the École de Boulangerie—and two years working for Papa—taught them everything there was to know, and now they are the

only women to have earned the respected diploma of Maître de Boulangerie. At La Flûte Gana they prepare country loaves, traditional pastries, and their popular baguettes. "The boulangerie is a passion, absolutely," says Isabelle. "The work is too hard, the hours too long to choose to do it without loving it. But the satisfactions are great—the look, the smell, the texture of fine bread, and the pleasure it brings to people."

BACON TARTLETS

Makes 6 servings

These little tarts reflect the original quiche from Lorraine, which was first baked in Nancy in the fifteenth century. Then, as now, the basic products of Lorraine were used—butter, eggs and smoked bacon. (Cheese was a later addition to the mix.)

BUTTER PASTRY:

1⅔ cups all-purpose flour
Pinch of salt
⅔ cup softened butter
4 to 5 tablespoons ice water

BACON FILLING:

¼ pound slab bacon, cut into ¼-inch cubes
2 eggs, plus 1 egg white
1 cup milk
½ cup crème fraîche or sour cream
Salt and pepper, to taste

TO MAKE THE BUTTER PASTRY:

1. In a medium-size bowl, combine the flour and salt. Cut in the butter until the mixture resembles a coarse meal. Sprinkle ice water over the flour mixture, a little at a time, tossing with a fork until the dough clings together.
2. Gather the dough into a ball. Form into a flat rectangular shape and wrap in plastic. Refrigerate for at least 1 hour.
3. Butter 6 round tartlet molds that measure 4 inches across the top and ¾ inch deep.
4. Cut the dough into 6 equal portions. On a lightly floured surface, roll out each portion of dough to a 6 inch circle and trim to a 5½-inch circle. Press the pastry into the prepared molds. Fold the edges of the dough over the side and crimp the edges.

5. Let the dough stand for 45 minutes, uncovered, to dry slightly.

TO MAKE THE BACON FILLING:

1. Preheat the oven to 375°F. In a medium-size skillet over medium heat, cook the bacon until browned. Drain on paper towels and set aside.
2. In a medium-size bowl, whisk together the eggs and egg white. Whisk in the milk, crème fraîche, and salt and pepper until well blended.
3. Sprinkle the bacon cubes evenly over bottom of the tarts. Pour the egg mixture into each mold, filling almost to the top. Arrange the molds on a baking sheet.
4. Bake for 50 to 60 minutes, until the tops are deep golden brown. Let stand on wire racks for 10 minutes before serving.

who had lost their aristocratic patrons began to serve up simple meals along with wine or beer. Nowadays restaurants range from a simple place owned by a husband and wife who may order in pastries, prepare a few specialties, and bring out the carafes for their patrons, to the grand and serious temples of dining with their serried ranks of staff, menus as large as billboards, and gourmands eyeing each new sauce with due consideration and attention. Diners rely on their Michelin guides—when French motorists first took to the roads at the turn of the century, being caught in a strange part of the world without a clue of where to eat must have been terrible—until the tire makers instituted the first of their red-covered volumes, and the star system, which calls

This sweet omelette, opposite, filled with apple slices flamed in Calvados, is airy perfection, gilded in butter. Traditionalists insist on a copper bowl and hand-whisking for proper loft to the eggs. Eggs at room temperature will achieve more lightness as well.

ELEGANT DESSERT OMELETTE

Makes 1 serving

The omelette is popular everywhere, prepared simply with *fines herbes* or cheese, or as a good background to luxurious ingredients like truffles or, as here, with apples.

3 tablespoons unsalted butter
1 apple, such as Granny Smith, peeled, cored, and sliced
1 to 2 tablespoons sugar, to taste
3 tablespoons Calvados
3 large eggs
1 teaspoon vanilla extract
Sliced apple, for garnish

1. In a skillet set over medium-high heat, melt 2 tablespoons of the butter. Add the apple and cook, stirring, for 5 minutes, or until softened. Sprinkle with the sugar and cook for 5 minutes more. Remove from the heat and stir in the Calvados. In a small bowl, whisk the eggs with the vanilla.

2. Set a 9-inch nonstick skillet over high heat. Add the remaining 2 tablespoons butter, swirling the pan to coat. When the bubbling subsides but before the butter starts to brown, pour in the eggs. With the back of a fork, stir the eggs in a circular motion while shaking the pan back and forth over the heat for 5 to 10 seconds, or until the eggs begin to coagulate. Add the apple filling, spreading evenly over the eggs, and fold the bottom third of the omelette to meet the center of the pan. Fold the top third of the omelette down over the bottom and invert the omelette onto a plate. Garnish with the sliced apples.

HAZELNUT AND CHOCOLATE TART

Makes 6 to 8 servings

The dessert trolley is rolled into view, and the choice is dazzling—which shall it be? Chocolate is a favorite, and this tart pairs it with the traditional hazelnuts and an almond crust.

ALMOND PASTRY:

1½ cups all-purpose flour

½ cup confectioners' sugar

2 tablespoons finely ground almonds

10 tablespoons (1¼ sticks) cold unsalted butter, cut into bits

1 large egg, beaten lightly

1 to 2 tablespoons ice water

GANACHE:

2 cups heavy cream

1 pound bittersweet chocolate, chopped

1 cup chopped toasted hazelnuts

Strawberries and toasted hazelnuts, for garnish

TO MAKE THE ALMOND PASTRY:

1. In a medium-size bowl, sift together the flour and confectioners' sugar. Add the almonds and butter and using a pastry blender or two knives blend the mixture until it resembles a coarse meal. Add the egg and enough ice water until the dough clings together. Form the dough into a disk, wrap in plastic, and chill for 30 minutes.
2. Preheat the oven to 350°F.
3. On a lightly floured surface, roll out the dough to a 12-inch round. Fit the dough into a 10-inch tart pan and trim the edges. Line the dough with waxed paper, weigh it with dried beans or rice, and bake for 20 minutes. Remove the dried beans and paper and bake for 5 to 10 minutes more, until the pastry is golden. Transfer to a wire rack to cool.

TO MAKE THE GANACHE:

1. In a saucepan set over medium heat, bring the cream to a simmer. Remove the pan from the heat, add the chocolate and stir the mixture until it is smooth. Transfer 1½ cups of the ganache mixture to a small bowl and chill. Stir the hazelnuts into the remaining ganache mixture. Pour the mixture into the pastry shell, and chill for 1 hour.
2. Chill the reserved ganache until firm enough to be piped, 30 to 45 minutes. Transfer the mixture to a pastry bag fitted with a large star tip and pipe the chocolate onto the tart in a decorative pattern. Before serving, garnish the tart with the strawberries and hazelnuts and let stand 10 minutes to soften.

CHEFS IN THE MAKING

Once the *grand-mère* was the young chef's tutor, teaching her charge to pay careful attention to the splattered pages of her recipe book. In a country so concerned with the table arts, beginning young was one way to become adept at hollandaise. Besides, those moments in the kitchen near the warm stove, watching butter and sugar and eggs and flour metamorphose into a cake to be eaten warm from the oven—what heaven in the memory. Lucky children still have this introduction, learning

to mince the garlic, chop the parsley, taste the soup. Very fortunate children, like young Alexandra Lorain, left, learn from their fathers. Hers happens to be three-star chef Jean-Michel, who loves to gather children about him in his kitchen in Joigny. "For them it's child's play; for me, it's passing on tradition," he says. To this end, he has written two cookbooks just for children—and, knowing children, he began with dessert. His *Desserts en Fête*, above, is a cheerfully illustrated guide to the classics, but made for children who can't keep their fingers out of the batter. "I can make my favorites all by myself," says his daughter Marine, who loves the apple cake scenting the air.

In Strasbourg, above, sweets like these feather-weight meringues are especially important. In all regions of the country, the most important culinary role is played by tradition: the handing down of family recipes, right.

attention to many a new chef and keeps the established ones on their mettle. Other occasions are just right for a café, which opens early and closes by around ten P.M. It's the ideal place for a glass of wine or spirits, a croque-monsieur, and a quiet corner in which to read the paper as the world parades by outside. Every neighborhood has a bistro or two (the word is Russian for "hurry," introduced into the language by French soldiers returning from the Napoleonic Wars). An informal restaurant with a traditional menu that has changed little in a hundred years, the bistro offers *blanquette de veau* and *steak pommes frites*, and a *crème caramel* waiting on the dessert tray. Modest prices, with a *plat du jour* offered each afternoon, can always be counted on. These establishments are full of the neighborhood's character—and characters. A brasserie is a more ambitious place. First created in the 1870s by refugees from Alsace, these are beautifully designed eating palaces offering full menus. A brasserie is often a grandiose eating hall of Belle Époque splendor, with glittering brasswork,

GÂTEAU DES ROIS

Makes 6 to 8 servings

The final feast of Christmas comes on Twelfth Night, with a special cake to mark the arrival of the Three Kings to Bethlehem. In the north, the cake is usually a marzipan-filled puff pastry; in the south, a yeast cake like this one is the choice.

YEAST CAKE:
¼ **ounce fast-rising yeast**
2 tablespoons warm (110°F-115°F) water
4 eggs
⅔ **cup granulated sugar**
½ **teaspoon salt**
1 tablespoon freshly grated orange zest
1 tablespoon orange flower water
2 cups all-purpose flour
½ **cup (1 stick) softened unsalted butter**

LEMON GLAZE:
1 cup confectioners' sugar
1 tablespoon fresh lemon juice
1 teaspoon orange flower water

¼ **cup coarsely chopped sugar cubes**
Candied fruit, for garnish

TO MAKE THE YEAST CAKE:
1. Butter a 9-inch springform pan with a center tube insert. Set aside.
2. In a small bowl, sprinkle the yeast over the water. Stir until dissolved.
3. In the large bowl of an electric mixer, beat the eggs, granulated sugar, salt, orange zest, and orange flower water at medium speed until well blended.
4. Gradually stir in the flour, butter, and yeast mixture with a wooden spoon just until the mixture is combined.

5. Spoon the batter into the prepared pan, spreading until smooth. Place the pan on a baking sheet. Cover the pan with a damp kitchen towel and let rise in warm place until doubled in bulk, about 1 hour. Preheat the oven to 400°F.
6. Bake for 10 minutes then reduce the oven temperature to 350°F. Continue baking for 20 minutes, or until golden brown.
7. Cool the cake in the pan set on a wire rack for 10 minutes. Remove the cake from the pan and cool on the rack. When cool, place the rack over waxed paper.

TO MAKE THE GLAZE:
1. In a small bowl, combine the confectioners' sugar, lemon juice, and orange flower water. Mix well and drizzle over the cake.
2. Sprinkle the glaze with chopped sugar cubes and garnish with candied fruit.

SIX-STAR CHEF

Evenings in Paris, the fortunate few have bookings at a grand restaurant, like that of Alain Ducasse. Dining in high style at his high-flying restaurant of the same name in Paris's Hôtel le Parc may be a once-in-lifetime experience, filled with ceremony and drama, of fine wines and dishes like those nowhere else. And Ducasse, who has been awarded more Michelin-awarded stars than anyone else in France, is the man of the moment. "Perhaps it's simply because I love to eat that I cook well," he says. Brought up on a farm where his parents raised geese and ducks for foie gras, the family feasted every Sunday. At sixteen he began an apprenticeship with a local restaurant, then worked in the kitchens of most of the best chefs of France, learning along the way. His talents were recognized early, as he set about creating a cuisine that was simple yet simply perfect. He'll concentrate on dishes that speak of their very essence, perhaps combining just two or three ingredients, a bit of salt, and surely some magic, for plate full of discovery for the diner. And so the sumptuous restaurant Alain Ducasse fills each evening with diners speaking in hushed tones as they unfold their broad linen napkins and reach for the menu, ready for the dazzlement provided by one of France's most remarkable and inventive chefs.

marble halls, and sparkling stained glass. Here, as in many of the cafés and restaurants, one can linger over one's lunch and conversation, as did philosophers like Simone de Beauvoir and Albert Camus and painters like Toulouse-Lautrec, Picasso, and Monet.

And the pleasure of dining out is shared by the whole family from the earliest years. On Sundays, platoons of families arrive religiously at the local restaurant and claim their tables for the afternoon. Small children learn early how to manage those clanking utensils and balance on their chairs; feet dangling, starched white napkins tucked under their chin, they try valiantly to manage each course as it arrives and to hold up their end of the conversation. Adults from each generation passionately debate politics and philosophy, music and art, or simply pass on the latest gossip and talk of the town. Glasses are raised, toasts are offered, and camaraderie triumphs. The communion of the table, the love of food and family, is celebration enough, as the youngest cradles his head on his arm and drifts off to sleep while the cheese platter is passed over his head.

Elegant and artful as a well-worked jewel, the Paris restaurant Ledoyen has been a favorite with locals and visitors for fine dining since the eighteenth century. Its tables are dressed with simple silver pieces and the whitest linens.

CONVERSION CHART

VOLUME

USA	METRIC
1 teaspoon	5 ml
1 tablespoon	15 ml
¼ cup	60 ml
⅓ cup	80 ml
½ cup	120 ml
⅔ cup	160 ml
¾ cup	180 ml
1 cup	240 ml
1 pint (U.S.)	475 ml
1 quart	.95 liter
1 quart plus ¼ cup	1 liter
1 gallon (U.S.)	3.8 liters

WEIGHT

USA	METRIC
1 ounce	28.3 grams
4 ounces	113 grams
8 ounces	227 grams
12 ounces	340.2 grams
1 pound	.45 kilo
2 pounds, 3¼ ounces	1 kilo (1,000 grams)

TEMPERATURE

(To convert from Fahrenheit
to Celsius: subtract 32, multiply by 5,
then divide by 9)

32°F	0°C
212°F	100°C
250°F	121°C
325°F	163°C
350°F	76°C
375°F	190°C
400°F	205°C
425°F	218°C
450°F	232°C

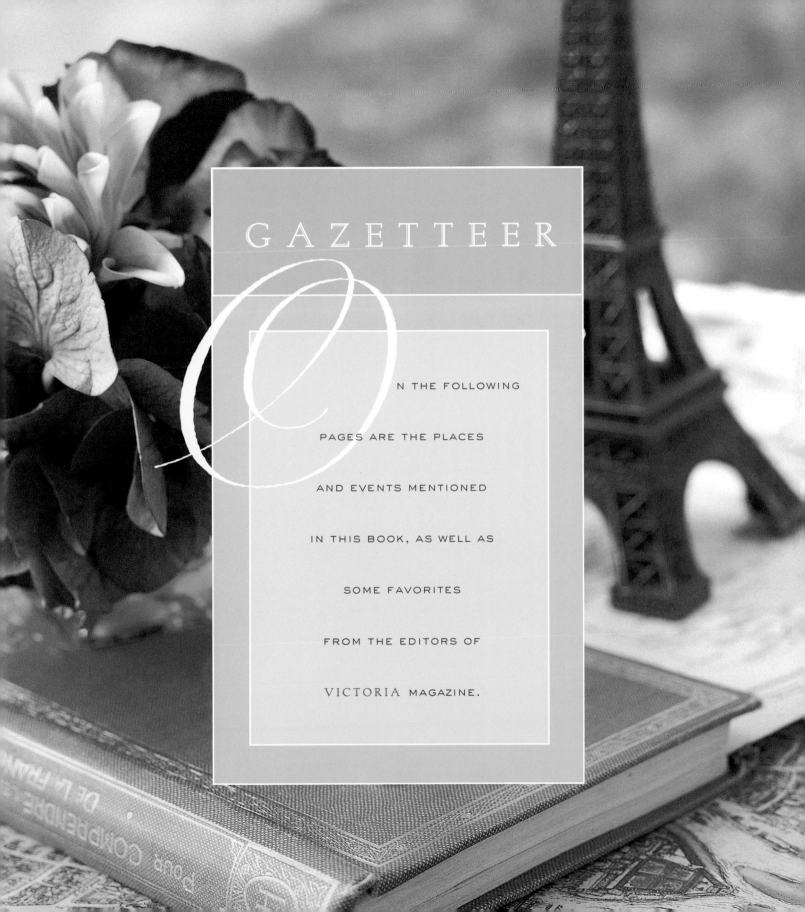

GAZETTEER

O N THE FOLLOWING

PAGES ARE THE PLACES

AND EVENTS MENTIONED

IN THIS BOOK, AS WELL AS

SOME FAVORITES

FROM THE EDITORS OF

VICTORIA MAGAZINE.

ADDRESS BOOK

To call France from the U.S.: dial
011 + 33 + the nine-digit number.
When in France, dial 0, then the
nine-digit number.

PLACES TO STAY

Auberge du Parc
Île de Fédrun
44720 Saint Joachim
tel: 240 88 53 01

Château de Vault-de-Lugny
11 rue du Château
89200 Avallon
tel: 386 34 07 86
www.vault-de-lugny-chateau.com

Hôtel Printania
5 Avenue George V
35801 Dinard
tel: 299 46 13 07

Les Fermes de Marie
Chemin de Riante Colline
74120 Mégève
tel: 450 93 03 10
www.fermesdemarie.com

Les Prés d'Eugénie
40320 Eugénie-les-Bains
Landes
tel: 558 05 06 07 (information)
tel: 558 05 05 05 (reservations)

PLACES TO VISIT

Alain Ducasse
Hôtel le Parc
59 Avenue Raymond Poincarré
75116 Paris
tel: 147 27 12 27
www.alain-ducasse.com

Auberge la Lucarne aux Chouettes
Quai Bretoche
89500 Villeneuve-sur-Yonne
tel: 386 87 18 26
www.lesliecaron-auberge.com

Blanc d'Ivoire
104 rue du Bac
75007 Paris
tel: 145 44 41 17

Cachemires &Cachemires
5 rue Jean Jaurès
33310 Lormont
tel: 556 31 74 74

Camélia blanc
113 Route de la Reine
92100 Boulogne-sur-Seine
tel: 146 04 45 76

Château de Baccarat
rue des Cristalleries
54120 Baccarat
tel: 820 32 22 22

Château de Canon
142700 Mezidon
Calvados
tel: 31 20 05 07
open Easter to mid-September

Château de Versailles
78000 Versailles
tel: 130 84 74 00
closed Mondays

Chez Suzelle
2 rue des Moulins
67000 Strasbourg
tel: 388 23 10 46
closed Mondays

Christian Tortu Boutique
6 Carrefour Odéon
75006 Paris
tel: 143 26 02 56

D. Porthault & Co.
18 Avenue Montaigne
75008 Paris
tel: 147 20 75 25

D. Rose
8 rue Manuel
75009 Paris
tel: 145 26 04 54

Fragonard
20 Boulevard Fragonard
06332 Grasse
tel: 493 36 44 65
www.fragonard.com
catalog available

Galérie Louise Nott —Salon de Thé
29 rue Carnot
13210 St.-Rémy-de-Provence
tel: 490 92 05 79

Guerlain Shop
68 Champs-Elysées
75008 Paris
tel: (800) 882-8820
tel: 145 62 52 57

Hermès Museum
24 rue du Fauburg-St.-Honoré
75008 Paris
tel: 140 17 47 17

Jardins du Luxembourg
5 Imp. Royar-Collard
75006 Paris
tel: 140 46 08 88

Lachaume Flower Shop
10 rue Royale
75008 Paris
tel: 142 60 59 74

La Côte Basque
St. Jacques
89300 Joigny

Ladurée
75 Avenue des Champs-Elysées
75008 Paris
tel: 140 75 08 75
and
16 rue Royale
75008 Paris
tel: 142 60 21 79

La Flûte Gana
226 rue des Pyrenées
75020 Paris
tel: 143 58 58 42 62

L' Assiette de Marie
1 rue Jaume Roux
13210 St.-Rémy-de-Provence
tel: 490 92 32 14

La Toque Blanche
rue Principale
78490 Les Mesnuls
tel: 234 86 05 55

Ledoyen
1 Avenue Dutuit
75008 Paris
tel: 153 05 10 01

Le Grande Véfour
17 rue de Beaujolais
75001 Paris
tel: 142 96 56 27

L'Epicerie de Marie
1 Place Isidor Gilles
13210 St.-Rémy-de-Provence
tel: 490 92 12 37

Le Rideau de Paris
32 rue du Bac
75007 Paris
tel: 142 61 18 56

Louis Vuitton Centre de Communication d'Asnières
tel: 147 91 00 13
by appointment only; not open to the general public

Maison des Gîtes de France
(national bed and breakfast association)
35 rue Godot-de-Mauroy
75439 Paris
tel: 149 70 75 75

Musée Colette
Château Saint-Sauveur-en-Puisaye
89520 Saint-Sauveur-en-Puisaye
tel: 386 45 61 95
closed Tuesdays

Musée International de la Chaussure
2 rue Sainte-Marie
26100 Romans-sur-Isère
tel: 475 05 51 51

Musée Rodin
77 rue de Varenne
75007 Paris
tel: 144 18 61 10
closed Mondays

Parc de Bagatelle
3 Avenue de la Parte D'Auteuil
75016 Paris
tel: 140 71 75 23
tours available

Pierre Frey
22 rue Royale
75008 Paris
tel: 149 26 04 77
2 showrooms in Paris

Portobello
56 rue Notre-Dame des Champs
75006 Paris
tel: 143 25 74 47

Roseraie du Val-de-Marne
rue Albert Watel
94240 l'Haÿ-les-Roses
tel: 143 99 82 80
open May–September

Stern
47 Passage des Panoramas
75002 Paris
tel: 145 08 86 45

Teinturerie de Luxe Huguet
47 Avenue Marceau
75016 Paris
tel: 147 23 81 39

Victoria en Provence
139 Cours Gambetta
84300 Cavaillon
tel: 490 71 72 05

The Wallpaper Museum
28 rue Zuber
68170 Rixheim
tel: 389 64 24 56

CALENDAR OF EVENTS

JANUARY
Paris fashion shows
Limoux Carnival

FEBRUARY
Menton Lemon Festival
Nice Carnival

MARCH
Monte-Carlo Festival of
   Contemporary Film Music

APRIL
Lourdes Sacred Music Festival
Easter celebrations
Paris Marathon
Le Mans Motorcycle Race

MAY
Cannes Film Festival
Grasse International Rose Show
Mâcon Wine Fair
Stes. Marie-de-la-Mer Gypsy
   Pilgrimage
Monaco Grand Prix
Nîmes Feria

JUNE
Strasbourg Music Festival
Les Imaginaires at
   Mont-St.-Michel
Chartres International
   Organ Festival
Noirlac Music Festival
Le Mans 24-hour Car Race
Chantilly Prix de Diane Hermès
   Horse Race

JULY
Tour de France
Aix-en-Provence Festival
Antibes Jazz Festival
Avignon Festival
Bastille Day celebrations— July 14th
Nice Jazz Festival
Quimper Fêtes de Cornouailles

AUGUST
Antibes International Fireworks
   Festival
Lorient Celtic Festival
Marciac Jazz Festival
Menton International Chamber
   Music Festival
Dijon Grape Harvest and Folk Fair
Bagnères de Luchon Flower
   Festival

OCTOBER
Dijon International
   Gastronomy Fair
Paris Motor Show
Paris Jazz Festival

NOVEMBER
Beaujolais Nouveau celebrations
Beaune Wine Auction

DECEMBER
Paris Boat Show
Strasbourg Christmas Market

FRENCH HOLIDAYS

(banks, post offices, and most galleries, museums, and stores closed)

January 1
Jour de l'An

Easter Sunday & Monday
Pâques

May 1
(Labor Day)
Fête du Travail

May 8
Victoire 1945

Ascension

Pentecost
Pentecôte

July 14
(Bastille Day)
Fête Nationale

August 15
Assomption

November 1
(All Saints' Day)
Toussaint

November 11
Armistice 1918

December 25
Noël

GENERAL RESOURCES

INFORMATION SOURCES

French Government Tourist Office
444 Madison Avenue
New York, NY 10022-6903
TEL. (212) 838-7800
FAX (212) 838-7855
www.francetourism.com

Air France
(800) 237-2747
www.airfrance.com

French Ministry of Culture . . . . www.culture.fr
French Embassy in the U.S. . . . . www.info-france-usa.org
Rail Europe . . . . www.raileurope.com
Eurostar . . . . www.eurostar.com
Paris Convention & Visitors Bureau . . . www.paris-touristoffice.com

MISCELLANEOUS

France is 6 hours ahead of E.S.T.
France uses the 24-hour clock.
No visa is necessary to travel from
    U.S. and Canada (passport is required).

AVERAGE TEMPERATURES:
winter: 15–50°F
summer: 65–85°F in the hottest areas
along the southern Atlantic and
Mediterranean coasts

FLYING TIME:
New York–Paris   7.5 hours
Chicago–Paris   9 hours
Los Angeles–Paris   11 hours
U.K.–Paris   1 hour

REGIONAL WEBSITES

Alsace . . . . www.tourism-alsace.com
Aquitaine . . . . www.cr-aquitaine.fr
Auvergne . . . . www.crt-auvergne.fr
Brittany . . . . www.brittanytourism.com
Burgundy . . . . www.burgundy-tourism.com
Corsica . . . . www.sitec.fr/corsica
Eastern France . . . . www.easternfrance.com
Franche-Comté . . . . www.interfrance.com
Ile-de-France . . . . www.paris-ile-de-france.com
Languedoc-Roussillon . . . . www.cr-languedocroussillon.fr/tourisme
Limousin . . . . www.cr-limousin.fr
Loire Valley . . . . www.loirevalleytourism.com
Lorraine . . . . www.cr-lorraine.fr
Normandy . . . . www.normandy-tourism.com
Pays-de-la-Loire . . . . www.cr-pays-de-la-loire.fr
Provence . . . . www.cr-paca.fr
Riviera-Côte d'Azur . . . . www.crt-riviera.fr

BOOKSHELF

All Paris: Tout Paris Source Guide *(Second Edition)*
Patricia Twohill Lown and
David Lown
The Palancar Company, 1999

Bistro Cooking
Patricia Wells
Workman Publishing, 1989

Burgundy Stars
William Echikson
Little, Brown and Company, 1995

Ducasse Flavors of France
Alain Ducasse and
Linda Dannenberg
Artisan, 1998

Edible France
Glynn Christian
Interlink, 1997

Encore Provence
Peter Mayle
Alfred Knopf, 1999

Exploring the Flea Markets of France: A Companion Guide for Visitors and Collectors
Sandy Price
Three Rivers Press, 1999

Food Lover's Companion to France
Marc and Kim Millon
Macmillan Travel, 1996

The Food Lover's Guide to France
Patricia Wells
Workman Publishing, 1987

The Food Lover's Guide to Paris *(Third Edition)*
Patricia Wells
Workman Publishing, 1993

French Gardens: A Guide
Barbara Abbs
Sagapress, 1994

The French Touch: Decoration and Design in the Most Beautiful Homes of France
Daphne De Saint Sauveur
Bulfinch Press, 1997

French Vineyards: The Complete Guide and Companion
Michael Busselle
Trafalgar Square, 1998

The French Way: Aspects of Behavior, Attitudes, and Customs of the French
Ross Steele
Passport Books, 1995

L'Atelier de Alain Ducasse
Jean-Françoise Revel
Hachette, 1998

Markets of Provence: A Culinary Tour of Southern France *(Volume I)*
Ruthanne Long
Collins Publishers San Francisco, 1996

The Most Beautiful Villages of France
Dominique Reperant
Thames & Hudson, 1990
(translated from the French by Augusta Audubert)

Paris Flea Market
Herbert J. M. Ypma
Stewart, Tabori & Chang, 1996

Portraits of France
Robert Daley
Little, Brown and Company, 1991

Provence
Marie-Ange Guillaume
Abbeville Press, 1993

Provence: A Country Almanac *(Revised & Updated)*
Louisa Jones
Stewart, Tabori & Chang, 1999

Provence: The Art of Living
Sara Walden
Stewart, Tabori & Chang, 1996

**Reckless Appetites:
A Culinary Romance**
Jacqueline Deval
Ecco Press, 1993

To Live in France
James Bentley
Thames & Hudson, 1997

Toujours Provence
Peter Mayle
Vintage Books, 1992

Tradition Evolution
Alain Ducasse
Minerva, 1999

**Traveller's Literary
Companion: France**
John Edmonson
Passport Books, 1997

**Undiscovered France:
An Insider's Guide to the
Most Beautiful Villages**
Brigitte Tilleray
Cassell, 1998

**Wines and Vineyards
of Character and
Charm in France**
Fodor's Travel Publications,
1998

A Year in Provence
Peter Mayle
Vintage Books, 1991

PHOTOGRAPHY CREDITS

1	Toshi Otsuki	46–51	Toshi Otsuki (all)	112–115	Nicolas Millet (all)
2	Tom Eckerle	52–53	Carlos Spaventa (both)	116–117	Christophe Dugied (both)
4–5	Pierre Hussenot	54–55	Christophe Dugied (all)	118	Guy Bouchet (both)
6–9	Toshi Otsuki (both)	56–57	Gloria Baker	119	Christophe Dugied (both)
10	Guy Bouchet	58–59	Carlos Spaventa (both)	120–125	Guy Bouchet (all)
12	Guy Bouchet (top)	60–61	Toshi Otsuki (both)	126	Marlene Wetherell
12	Toshi Otsuki (bottom)	62	Guy Bouchet (both)	126–127	Guy Bouchet
13	Guy Bouchet (top)	63	William Steele (top)	128–131	Guy Bouchet (all)
13	Carlos Spaventa (bottom)	63	Nicolas Millet (bottom)	132	Peter Knaup (both)
14	Toshi Otsuki (bottom)	64–65	Gloria Baker (all)	133	Steve Cohen
14	Maurice Rougemont (top)	66–71	Guy Bouchet (all)	134–136	Pierre Hussenot (all)
15	Hugh Palmer (bottom)	72–73	Carlos Spaventa (both)	137	Christopher Drake (both)
15	Guy Bouchet (top)	74–76	Guy Bouchet (all)	138–139	Pierre Hussenot (both)
16	Guy Bouchet (top)	77	Nana Watanabe (both)	140–141	Guy Bouchet (both)
16	Toshi Otsuki (bottom)	78–81	Maurice Rougemont (all)	142–143	Nicolas Millet (both)
17	Laura Resen (top)	82	Toshi Otsuki	144–145	Hugh Palmer (all)
17	Guy Bouchet (bottom)	83	Flammarion	146	Joel Laiter
18	Tom Eckerle (bottom)	84–85	Toshi Otsuki (both)	147	Tom Eckerle
18	Pierre Hussenot (top)	86	Hugh Palmer (both)	148	Guy Bouchet (all)
19	Guy Bouchet (bottom)	87–93	Toshi Otsuki (all)	149	Pierre Hussenot
19	Nicolas Millet (top)	94–95	Pierre Chanteau (both)	150–151	Guy Bouchet (both)
20–21	Pierre Hussenot	96	Marlene Wetherell (left)	152–153	Pierre Hussenot (all)
22–23	Guy Bouchet (both)	96	Guy Bouchet (right)	154–155	Steven Randazzo (both)
24–25	Daniel Aubry (all)	97	Toshi Otsuki	156	Pierre Chanteau
26	Guy Bouchet (both)	98–101	Guy Bouchet (all)	157–158	Pierre Hussenot (all)
27	Laura Resen (both)	102–103	Toshi Otsuki (both)	159	Nicolas Millet
28–29	Guy Bouchet (both)	104–105	Nicolas Millet (all)	160	Guy Bouchet (both)
30–31	Carlos Spaventa (both)	106–107	Pierre Hussenot (all)	161	Hugh Palmer (both)
32–35	Guy Bouchet (all)	108	Toshi Otsuki (top)	162	Jean-Bernard Naudin
36–37	Christopher Drake (both)	108	William Steele (bottom)	163	Jim Bastardo
38	Luciana Pampalone (both)	109	Guy Bouchet (both)	166	Nana Watanabe
39	Pierre Hussenot (both)	110	Christophe Dugied (both)	169	Laura Resen
40–45	Guy Bouchet (all)	111	Laura Resen	171–176	Guy Bouchet (both)

INDEX

l'assiette de Marie

~ restaurant ~

92.92.32.16